My Neighbor Was a Serial Killer

A Writer's Memories of
Mayhem, Romance, and Murder

Robert U. Montgomery

My Neighbor Was a Serial Killer
A Writer's Memories of Mayhem, Romance, and Murder
Robert U. Montgomery
RUM Publishing

Published by RUM Publishing, Bonne Terre, MO
Copyright ©2021 Robert U. Montgomery
All rights reserved.

No part of this publication may be reproduced, stored in a retrieval system, or transmitted in any form or by any means, electronic, mechanical, photocopying, recording, scanning, or otherwise, except as permitted under Section 107 or 108 of the 1976 United States Copyright Act, without the prior written permission of the Publisher. Requests to the Publisher for permission should be addressed to Permissions Department, RUM Publishing, roticomontgomery@gmail.com

Names, characters, businesses, places, events and incidents are either the products of the author's imagination or used in a fictitious manner. Any resemblance to actual persons, living or dead, or actual events is purely coincidental.

Project Management and Book Design: DavisCreative.com

Publisher's Cataloging-In-Publication Data
(Prepared by The Donohue Group, Inc.)

Names: Montgomery, Robert U., author.

Title: My neighbor was a serial killer : a writer's memories of mayhem, romance, and murder / Robert U. Montgomery.

Description: Bonne Terre, MO : RUM Publishing, [2021]

Identifiers: ISBN 9781733003353 (paperback) | ISBN 9781733003360 (ebook)

Subjects: LCSH: Montgomery, Robert U. | Authors, American--20th century--Diaries. | Serial murderers--United States. | LCGFT: Diaries. | Autobiographies. | BISAC: BIOGRAPHY & AUTOBIOGRAPHY / Personal Memoirs. | TRAVEL / Special Interest / Adventure. | TRUE CRIME / Murder / Serial Killers.

Classification: LCC PS3613.O548835 Z46 2021 (print) | LCC PS3613. O548835 (ebook) | DDC 813/.6 B--dc23

ATTENTION CORPORATIONS, UNIVERSITIES, COLLEGES AND PROFESSIONAL ORGANIZATIONS: Quantity discounts are available on bulk purchases of this book for educational, gift purposes, or as premiums for increasing magazine subscriptions or renewals. Special books or book excerpts can also be created to fit specific needs. For information, please contact Robert U. Montgomery, RUM Publishing, roticomontgomery@gmail.com, http://rumpublishing.com.

Dedication

*With much affection,
this book is dedicated to
Sue, Sunny, Ellie, and Mary,
as well as to Grace, Doug,
and the girls.*

Table of Contents

Prologue 1

Part I:
   My Great Adventure 5

Part II:
   Home for the Holidays 55

Part III:
   Mono and Mayhem 69

Part IV:
   My Neighbor Was a Serial Killer 127

Epilogue. 191

About the Author. 201

Prologue

Yes, there's a serial killer in this story, along with a Hollywood producer, an adventure in Europe, and my introduction into a life of crime by the daughter of a prominent actor. It's a true story too.

I present it to you as journal entries, almost exactly as I wrote them more than 40 years ago. I have added a little clarification as to who's who and cleaned up a few spelling and punctuation errors. Also, I've changed some names out of respect for the privacy of those people.

Otherwise, this is a truthful account of the adventures and misadventures I experienced after my divorce in 1976.

Although I was 28 at the time this occurred, I was always years behind my peers in terms of landmark life events. I didn't even date in high school. I didn't get my driver's license until I was 18. And when I got married at age 24, I probably was closer to 18 or 19 in terms of maturity.

I'd always been a "good boy" too. I didn't drink in high school or take drugs. I made good grades and never got into trouble. In other words, I was an exemplary Baby Boomer—go to college, serve your country, find a job, get married, have kids…

Only my wife and I never got to that last part. During the first two years of marriage, we moved around, searching for a place where we both could find good jobs. But when we finally found that place—Tallahassee, Fla.—achieved the American Dream and settled into a routine, the relationship began to deteriorate. At least I think that's what happened. I still was the good boy and mostly oblivious. I almost certainly would have stayed married if Lois had not taken the first step.

But she told me that she was bored and depressed. By implication, even someone as oblivious as I was could see that she believed I was the reason for her unhappiness. She said she wanted a divorce.

Fortunately, Florida had what was called back then "no-fault" divorce, and that's the path we chose. I gave her everything, including the car, and moved into an apartment. I also continued to work as a newspaper features writer.

But slowly I began to realize that I was in a place that I'd never been before. I had fulfilled all obligations and, from this point, there was no societal road map to guide my behavior.

In other words, I was free!

The first thing I did was buy a totally impractical car, an MGB convertible with stick shift. Mostly it was impractical because I'd never driven a stick. So I taught myself.

Not long after, I decided that I'd go to Europe. I'd always thought about visiting there someday, especially Paris. For reasons I couldn't explain—and still can't—I'd always been drawn to that city. So my plan was to buy a Eurail pass and a French-English translation guide, strap on a backpack, and have an adventure!

Part I of this book is about that European adventure and exploration of my inexplicable attraction to Paris. It features a little romance, but mostly is about what I saw and experienced as I met new friends and traveled with them through France, Spain, and Great Britain, with brief stops in Monaco and Andorra.

Part II is about my first Christmas back home with my small-town family in about a decade. And, yes, there's romance—and sex—here as well.

Part III is where mono and mayhem join romance upon my return to Florida. I became ill the day I arrived back in the Sunshine State and, consequently, spent weeks confined to a rental bed in friends' living room. Not long after, I committed a crime and fled the scene, and, in revealing this, hope that the statute of limitations has run out. This part also is about Hollywood, good friends, and summer at the lake.

Part IV is the most serious in tone, dealing with loss, addiction, and murder by someone who I'd later learn was one of the nation's most notorious serial killers. But it also features a little sex, some special brownies, and a quirky adventure with a theater crowd as I struggle to decide what I want to do when I grow up.

*****

As I read the journal entries for the first time since I wrote them, I was often surprised by the difference between what I thought I remembered and what I put on paper. Sometimes, my memories were simply wrong. As a small example, I remembered that the father of a friend with whom I traveled in Europe ran an airline. Actually, he was president of a bank.

Other times, as I thought about it, I could see how I had blended two separate incidents into one memory.

Most frustrating was when I read about people I knew then that I have no memory of now.

Finally, should anyone I mention read about themselves in this book and say, "That's not what happened," I'll understand. Even when we simultaneously share experiences and adventures, our memories of what happened are not the same.

But this is what happened as I remember it.

Part I:
My Great Adventure

Nov. 9, 1976, Paris, France

I made it!

Here I sit in my hotel room on the Left Bank in Paris! I share it with a single-size bed, a sink, a hook on the back of the door for clothes, and what looks like a pan for soaking your feet but I suspect is a bidet. Then again, I don't know what a bidet is for. Maybe it is for soaking feet.

Bathroom is at the end of the hall.

Assessing my accommodations reminds me of "This Hotel Room," a new Jimmy Buffett song. But mine are considerably more Spartan than what he describes.

Why am I here? I can't tell you with any certainty. I don't speak French. I know little about French history. But for years, I've felt drawn here. Now maybe I'll find out why.

Before my divorce just a few months ago, Lois and I talked about coming here together. When I told her I was coming, she said that she envied me and that she never could do something like that.

"That" meant quitting a good job—as a columnist and features writer for a daily newspaper—selling nearly everything I owned, including my guitar, putting everything else in storage at my parents' house, and buying an open-ended ticket to Paris. A guy paid me $40 in two-dollar bills for my guitar, which I received in trade for a .22 rifle when I was in high school. I hated to sell the little Gibson, but the money helped me buy a camera for this adventure.

The only assistance I have is Arthur Frommer's ***Europe on $10 a Day*** and a French-English translation book given to me by a former neighbor. Arthur got me to this hotel—after I walked the streets for about an hour right at dusk, trying to figure out the lay of the land. I probably should have been frightened out of my mind, I guess. Lost, alone, and unable to speak the language. But I wasn't. Go figure.

Arthur also told me to take the train from Orly airport into Paris and then hop a bus to the Left Bank. He didn't tell me that I was supposed to go through customs as I left the airport or, if he did, I forgot. So, basically I just stepped off the plane with my camera bag and carry-on, walked out of the airport, got on the train, and no one said a word—or shot me. Only after I was on the bus did I realize what I had done.

Well, now I know that God does look out for fools, as well as children.

After checking in, I had my first meal in France at a little sidewalk café. Cheese and wine, of course, with a little crusty bread. Obviously recognizing me as an American, the waiter asked if I wanted a cheese "sandweech." I said, "non."

I'm so keyed up right now about the big unknown that awaits me, I feel like I'm not going to sleep for days. So why not just write some more? It's not like I have a TV to lull me to sleep as I would in an American hotel room. A couple of glasses of French red wine did nothing to take the edge off either.

Why am I here? Well, as I think about it, I remember that I do like the impressionists, especially Monet and Van Gogh. I probably was the only guy in the Army who had a Monet print of sailboats on the barracks wall above his bed. In Paris, I'll get to see the originals, along with other works of art at the Louvre.

Also, I fancy myself a writer. And isn't Paris a place for writers? Maybe that's the reason—or at least part of the reason—I'm here. So far, I've just written newspaper and a couple of magazine articles, but I'd like to write books one day. And if Paris was the place to come for Hemingway, Fitzgerald, Gertrude Stein, and others… Maybe this is where I will find inspiration.

What I do know is that being here on my own, with no ties to the past and no prospects for the future—just living in the now—feels like the first conscious decision that I've ever made in terms of what

I want to do with my life. Yeah, I guess that sounds crazy, but it's the way I feel.

Growing up, I always was a "good boy." I'm not suggesting that's a bad thing, but being one meant that I always did what was expected of me. And I didn't do it with any resentment or wish that I could do otherwise either. I just did it. Hell, I didn't even realize I was doing it either.

I made good grades and won all kinds of honors in high school. I did the same in college, where I majored in journalism, without really knowing why. Honestly, I never gave any thought to what I was going to do with a journalism degree until I was required to choose a specialization and I opted for editorial.

After college, I also did what was expected of me. I served in the Army. After being honorably discharged, I got my first job. And, with that out of the way, I—what else?—got married.

If Lois hadn't decided that she was unhappy and I was at the top of her reasons why, I almost certainly would have continued with the marriage too, never thinking about whether I was happy or unhappy. Instead, I just would have continued being a "good boy."

Wow! What a revelation. Thank you, French wine!

That divorce finally freed me to think for myself and do what I wanted to do, which was come to Paris. That's right. I think that coming here is the first major decision of my life that I truly made on my own, with no regard for social pressure or what I was supposed to do or what anyone else might think.

Now, if I can only figure out why I did it. On the other hand, why is that necessary? Why not just enjoy the ride?

Yes, that's what I'll do: Enjoy the ride.

I'm still not sleepy. But on that satisfactory note of self-discovery, I think that I'll lie back and rest my eyes on this, my first night in the City of Lights.

Nov. 17, Paris

Aw, Hell! I arrived in Paris more than a week ago and will leave for Nice tomorrow. Why oh why didn't I keep a daily accounting of what I've been doing here? During the train ride, I must try to remember and record my thoughts and experiences of my too brief stay in the City of Lights. Paris is everything I expected it to be and was a grand way to begin my trip. I've already made a half-dozen friends from three countries, at least two of whom I hope to see again.

On my first morning at breakfast in the hotel, I met like-minded people and haven't been alone since. That's a wonderful enhancement to my adventure that I never anticipated.

Nov. 19, Nice

Well, I didn't write on the train. It was too bumpy.

A little old lady met Alessio and me at the Nice train station and took us to the Hotel de France. Rate is 15 Francs ($3) a night. Every time a train goes by, the beds move and the whole room rattles. It's a scene right out of an old "I Love Lucy" episode.

On the way back from dinner, I was assaulted by a large dog of indiscriminate breed that tried to rape my leg. Speaking of dogs, their waste is all over the streets in Paris. That was a disappointment. And, while I'm on that subject, a little kid pulled down his pants and took a leak last night in the middle of the Paris train station, as his mother watched in approval. Based on their dress, they were Africans, I think.

Ronda was supposed to come with us to Nice. Yesterday morning, she received a letter from a guy in Germany whom she had traveled with. He has the clap, and accused her of giving it to him. She's still in Paris, awaiting test results. If she has it, she said, odds are she got it from him because a guy she had lived with reported in healthy when she called back home to New Orleans. And odds are that neither Alessio nor I will be pursuing that romantic encounter if/when she does join us.

Ronda is a Jewish American Princess with a lot of problems—besides the clap. She's extremely bright, but terribly insecure. Within five minutes, she's told you her life story—law student from Pittsburgh; rich, divorced parents; boyfriend her parents didn't approve of; father sent her to Europe to get her away from boyfriend, etc.

And while I and most of the travelers I've met carry our stuff in backpacks and/or shoulder bags, she drags around a large pink trunk that her father gave her for the trip. More accurately, guys—like Alessio and me—drag it for her.

In addition to Alessio and Ronda, I also met Rich and Kris. Rich and I met because we wound up in the same room at that little hotel on the Left Bank, after I was moved to one with two beds. I was in one of them when he unlocked the door and stepped in. Evidently, $10 gets you a room share, not a room, along with that bath at the end of the hall.

Rich is from Saratoga Springs, N.Y. He recently was divorced after six years of marriage and two children. He came to Europe to forget and get his head together, he said. On the same day he was served a divorce summons, he lost his insurance job.

"You know, it's funny," he told me. "I used to drive along, thinking how I was unhappy in my marriage and didn't like my job. But I probably wouldn't have done anything about either. Then this happened."

Now he has another chance. Will he allow himself to become entrapped in other circumstances where he's not happy? I could ask myself the same question.

Rich seems determined not to. But I think he's a role player, and, happy or not, soon will be a husband, father, and provider again. Wow. Does that sound pompous of me? But that's what I think. Of course, maybe he suspects the same about me.

Meanwhile, Alessio is from Toronto. He was born in Italy, but spent much of his life in Peru, where his father is director of a bank. He's a very easy going and likeable person, and we seem to get along well together. He speaks French, Spanish, and Italian too! We'll probably go to Barcelona together also.

Kris is from Seattle. She studied to be a journalist, but really hasn't used her education. Mostly, I think, she's worked at odd jobs, making just enough to do what she wants. I was very attracted to her, and tempted to go with her to Italy. But because I was so attracted to her, I didn't go. I want to go my own way for awhile and meet even more people who are doing the same. I came to Europe for an adventure, not to rebound into another relationship. I really hope to see Kris again, though, maybe in Washington.

*****

The most impressive thing about Paris for me was the architecture, especially Notre Dame. The ancient cathedral was something that I had not anticipated, and it was magnificent. One chilly night, we went to an organ concert there. If the church has any form of heating, it wasn't noticeable. But a little discomfort was a small price to pay for the extraordinary experience of enjoying Christmas music in one of the most historic structures in the world.

I loved seeing the gargoyles too. These magnificent monsters frighten away evil forces from the church and its community—or so I was told. They also serve a more practical purpose, acting as water spouts to allow water to run off the roof without damaging the walls.

Four of us had lunch under the Eiffel Tower one day, and then went to the top to survey Paris from more than 1,000 feet up. My favorite thing about the Tower, though, was watching it sparkle at night.

Another day we packed some wine, cheese, olives, and crusty bread, hopped on a bus, and went to the Palace of Versailles. We didn't go for a picnic. We went to see what was once the royal residence of France. Kings lived there, as did Marie Antoinette until she lost her head. But we thought it wise to take along our own food.

I'm so glad we did. The halls, the paintings, the sculptures, and the fountains were extraordinary, for sure. And it's difficult to comprehend that most of this opulence was just part of everyday life for kings and queens of France. But picnicking in the gardens unquestionably was the highlight—at least for me.

Possibly because of the time of year. Possibly because of the cool, cloudy weather. Possibly because it was a weekday. Or possibly because supernatural forces were at work. But for whatever the reason, few other people were in the palace, and we had the gardens totally to ourselves! It was like we owned the place. Rather, it was like I owned the place.

Yeah, I know how that sounds. But what it felt like to me was that I had invited friends over for a picnic in my gardens.

I have no idea why, but as I said before, I've always been drawn to Paris. That being the case, you'd think that I would have studied French in college instead of Spanish. But I didn't. I guess that means the attraction isn't about the language for me or maybe even the culture. Yeah, maybe it's about Paris being a writer's city. But the familiarity that I felt during the picnic is an entirely new link that I'd never been conscious of before. Maybe this attraction is about more than just one city. Maybe it's about Versailles too and, by extension, the entire country and its people.

Well, that's enough Twilight Zone stuff for now. Before we boarded the bus to return to Paris, we stopped into a little café for coffee. I don't know what kind of restroom facilities were available for the women, but they consisted of a hole in the floor in the men's room, suggesting the building was around long before the advent of indoor plumbing. Can't help but wonder what kind of facilities Louis and Marie had at the palace. And just how deep is that hole, anyway?

Back in Paris, we frequented a café that did have indoor plumbing. It also had a jukebox. I can't remember which one of us started it, but every time we were there, we played "Whiter Shade of Pale" by Procol Harum over and over and over. That's one of the seemingly inconsequential things about this trip that I suspect I will remember forever, like the smell of Coast soap in the shower at the hotel where we are staying.

Food was okay in the café, and most every place we dined. The best we had, ironically, was Greek and Chinese. But I did love the local soups and pastries, as well as the cheeses. I would have tried escargot had I found it on any of the menus. But I did sample coquilles Saint Jacques—scallops poached in white wine, atop mushrooms—and loved it.

We sometimes indulged in the pastries before our meals, after considerable window-shopping at the bakeries. Crusty baguettes were awesome too. Every day I saw dozens of people on bikes, carrying a loaf or two in their wire baskets. That's one of the visions that I'll remember most from Paris.

Along with coffee, hot chocolate, and cheese, breakfast at the hotel featured wonderful, flaky croissants, as well as classical music for our dining pleasure. The hotel seemed to be a favorite of European tourists, but Americans not so much, although that's where I met Rich, Kris, Ronda, as well as Alessio.

During my first real meal at a restaurant in Paris, sitting at a community table with strangers, I ordered fish for dessert, as I attempted to read from the menu. But a compassionate waitress knew what I intended, despite my atrocious French, and kindly explained the difference in broken English. In general, I found the people in Paris to be friendly and helpful if I made an honest attempt to communicate with them in their language, instead of just speaking slowly and loudly in English in hope that would help them understand me. I couldn't believe how many times I saw clueless Americans do that. It was embarrassing.

I carry a translation book with me. But even with that, it doesn't always turn out so well. One afternoon, a half dozen small children ran up to me as I walked along the Left Bank. Clearly they were excited, and they all starting speaking—French, of course—at the same time. I had no clue what they were telling me. So referring to the book and replying in what I thought was passable French, I said, "I don't under you. I'm an American."

That silenced them immediately and they quickly ran on down the street. But just a few yards away, one of them stopped, turned, and yelled, "Auf wiedersehen!" I'm not sure if he was sincere, and my French was that bad, or if he was just having fun with me. But he did have a twinkle in his eye.

The weather was lousy, gray and cloudy every day. Mums in the Tuileries Garden provided much welcome color—until workers started removing them in preparation for winter. And that concludes my Paris report.

In hindsight, I probably should have kept up with this journal every night so I could provide more details about my adventures. But my rationale is that I came to experience, not to write about the experience. Still, decades from now, it will be fun to read what I've written here and relive the trip. Can't guarantee anything, but I'll try to do a better job of keeping up with what's going on day to day.

*****

The ultimate freedom that unplanned travel like this offers is still hard to grasp. But it's really fun trying to get hold of it. Part of it is doing what you want when you want, like going to a pastry shop before dinner or staying an extra long time at one place—like the impressionist museum—because you like it, and not feeling guilty because you don't get to another place you'd planned to see that day.

The people you meet seem more honest and open than most in the real world. Perhaps the reason is these are once-in-a-lifetime meetings and paths probably never will cross again. As a consequence, barriers are dropped temporarily. I like to think they're honest and open because they're special people, people who aren't afraid to pack up and go off to see the world and share their thoughts and lives with others.

It's still wondrous to me that I'm seeing the things I'm seeing and visiting a country where every man, woman, and child speaks French. It's difficult to comprehend a place where people live and die, eat and sleep, love and hate, yet don't speak the same language I do. It's sort of a blow to the ego, I guess, to realize there's a world out there where I know almost nothing of what's going on—at least verbally. But at the same time, it's exciting.

Nov. 22, Nice

We've spent a lot of time near and on the beach here, as well as visited two modern art museums. The one we saw yesterday is near the ancient, walled city of Saint Paul. The highlight of the day, though, was the return bus trip.

Alessio and I boarded a bus filled with uniformed French school girls and a couple of nuns. For the entire trip back to Nice, they serenaded us. With their rich, pure, adolescent voices, they sang in French, of course, but I recognized most of the songs, including "Working on the Railroad" and "Do-Re-Mi," which made it seem as if we were participating in a sequel to *Sound of Music*. Another was "Old Stewball," which seemed especially appropriate. As I remember it in English, the lyrics go something like this: "He never drank water; he always drank wine."

Finally, as we rolled into Nice, they sang "Dominique," the song popularized by the Singing Nun back in the 1960s. It was awesome!

*****

At the beach today, Alessio and I shared a bottle of wine for lunch—another benefit of being a vagabond. It seemed more potent than other wines we'd had and sent both of us reeling for awhile there. How do the French do it? Drink so much wine and still go about their everyday activities, I mean. Or is that just a stereotype?

We're continually meeting Canadians, and only rarely anyone from the United States. Many of them seem to be on some sort of endurance trip—one day here, two days there, etc. I'm really glad I'm doing it at a more leisurely pace.

As I become more comfortable with the little French I've learned, I'm starting to enjoy ordering in restaurants, and I feel 10 feet tall when I hear other English-speaking people ordering in English or pointing at the menu. Going into a restaurant for the first time alone, I think, was my major phobia upon arriving in France. It seems rather ironic how something you once feared can change into a fun experience.

Nov. 24, Nice

Déjà vu. Yesterday, we spent another day at the beach, which along the French Riviera is gravel and rock, not sand. I was strolling along the waterline, minding my own business, when I happened to look up the beach and saw Ronda and about a half-dozen guys from California (I later learned).

Ronda doesn't have the clap after all.

The three of us rented motor bikes for the day to sightsee along the coast. First, Ronda fell off her bike going down a steep hill. Later, she ran into me while Alessio and I were talking to four girls on the boardwalk in Monaco. The coup de grace came during rush hour in Monte Carlo.

Ronda lost control of her bike going up a hill and fell in the middle of the highway. A bus going the other way missed her by inches. I was behind her and had to raise my bike up on its back wheel and bounce onto the sidewalk to avoid being part of the accident About 50 cars behind me slammed on their brakes and Ronda escaped with minor cuts and bruises.

Traveling back after dark, the lights went out on my bike. We were motoring single file and I moved up between Rhonda and Alessio for semi-protection. About halfway back from Monaco, a policeman stepped out of the darkness and pulled over Alessio and me. Ronda sped on down the road, oblivious to the fact we had been stopped.

Uh, oh, we're going to the slammer, I thought. But Alessio worked his magic. We still were detained for about an hour, while the policeman wrote a multipage report and told us to sign it. But then he allowed us to continue on our way to Nice.

When we finally pulled into the bike rental business, Ronda reported tearfully that her last fall had broken her gas tank, and she ran out of fuel just outside Nice. Fortunately, the bikes can be pedaled, and that's the way she made it into town, scared to death, of course, when she found out she was alone.

Highlights of the trip were seeing the Oceanographic Museum, where Jacque Cousteau is the director, seeing the changing of the guard at the palace, and eating Grand Marnier crepes, purchased from a street vendor. They were messy, but marvelous. Seeing the lights of the French Riviera as we wound along the coastal road was a real treat too. I stopped at an overlook just outside Nice to take photos.

Monaco is a storybook place. The palace is on top of a mountain, overlooking a beautiful harborful of yachts and sailboats.

*****

Also today, Ronda lost her traveler's checks. Alessio and I now are pondering what tragedy is going to befall her next, and starting to fear that if we stay around her long enough, we're going to get caught up in the melodrama, something we definitely do *not* want.

Upon her arrival in Amsterdam, Ronda had her wallet stolen. Then there was a pregnancy scare. Then the clap clamor.

Nov. 25, Nice

Today—surprise!—we relaxed at the beach, people watching, feeding seagulls, drinking wine and eating baguettes and squid salad. At least Alessio said that is what it was, and it did look a bit like chicken salad. Whatever it was, it was tasty. The gulls preferred the bread. Lying on our backs after eating and drinking our first bottle of wine, we tossed chunks into the air and watched the birds swoop down to grab them. I lay down beneath the feeding frenzy and took crooked photos of them directly overhead. In hindsight, I'm not so sure that was a good idea. But I got lucky, I guess. Note to self: Don't do that again.

As I relaxed there after the bread was gone, I locked my hands behind my head and looked up at the biggest and bluest sky I had ever seen. Gazing at its grandeur, I had an overwhelming sense of self-awareness about where I was at that moment in time—a small-town American country boy, soaking up the sun on the French Riviera. And I felt so happy that I had the courage to get on that plane and come to Europe alone.

"This is the best," I said to Alessio.

Alessio laughed and replied, "Yeah, except for that."

When I looked up, he was pointing at a naked fat man about 100 yards away.

That's when I realized that people here are much less inhibited about their appearances than in the states—maybe because they're drinking so much wine. Women lie topless on their blankets. Both sexes dress and undress in public. After much deliberation, I'm fine with that, although I'd vote for maximum age and weight limits. Some things seen never can be unseen.

I don't want to join in on the "fun" either, thank you.

On the way back from the beach, Alessio and I turned up one street where we saw a mother helping her little boy piss near a car wheel. Up the street a few yards, another mother was holding her daughter up by the legs so she could relieve herself.

Alessio and I both lamented we hadn't found that street a few minutes before. We had just paid 10 centimes each to use a public toilet.

UCLA sweaters are a hot item in Nice, it seems. We saw them everywhere, but especially in and around the colorful flower and produce markets. I loved walking among the bouquets and inhaling the intoxicating fragrances. The produce market, with lots of plucked chickens and ducks, not so much.

We also noted that women often walk arm-in-arm here, just as they do in Paris.

Nov. 26, Barcelona, Spain

That previous entry was interrupted by Brenda and Sue, two girls from Edmonton, Alberta, Canada. The four of us went out for grog, a hot rum drink on a cool night, during our last night in Nice.

They also came to Barcelona with us, as did Frederico, an unemployed architect from Chicago. Ronda stayed in Nice.

Barcelona is a gray city. Everything, streets, buildings, sky, appears to have been carved out of the same gray granite. It seemed that way when we arrived last night. And it seems that way again today, quite a contrast from Nice, a composite of bright colors, where blue waters brush white cliffs covered in green vegetation and stacked high with pink and white buildings.

Both Sue and Brenda are unemployed too. The former is a nurse; the latter is a physiotherapist. Frederico, who boarded our train at Perpignon, near the Spanish border, was born in Mexico and studied architecture in Mexico City. He had dual citizenship, but renounced his U.S. citizenship to avoid the military. Both he and Alessio speak fluent Spanish and it really makes getting about the city easier.

Frederico would have arrived in Spain before us, had he not been stopped at the border. He has a Mexican passport, and, ironically, Mexican nationals cannot enter Spain without a visa. Like me, he's recently divorced. He's a friendly guy, but doesn't talk much about himself, quite a contrast from Ronda.

Ronda reminds me of misfortune, which reminds me of something Sue said to her: "The bad things that are happening to you could happen anywhere, even at home. But the good things, the experiences you're having, could only happen because you're travelling, going places, and meeting people."

We're all staying at the Hotel Corello, a clean, well kept place with brass beds, near the old part of Barcelona. It's only a few minutes from the Ramblas, a broad promenade. Bars are all over the place. As we strolled by one last night, we heard Glenn Miller's "Moonlight Serenade." That drew us inside, to a setting right out of a 1940s movie. The smoke-filled air had a golden cast to it. Sawdust and peanut shells littered the floor. Mostly couples sat at the small, round tables, while rough-looking men stood at the bar. Drinks for five cost us less than $5.

Police and soldiers are all over the place in Barcelona. Some carry machine guns. It's sort of frightening to be in such a militaristic place. The girls said they saw the same thing in Italy, except the uniforms were more flamboyant.

Alessio tells me all sorts of bad things about Italy. But he says them with a special sort of affection for his homeland. He says to hold on tight to your wallet in Italy. But if it gets stolen, don't worry about any important papers in it. Italian thieves are gentlemen; they take only the money and return the rest. He also tells Italian jokes, such as:

"What's the difference between an elephant and an Italian mother-in-law?"

Answer: "About 50 pounds."

Italian drivers scare him to death, he insists, because their first rule of driving is "what's behind me doesn't matter."

But the wonderful food, he proclaims, makes enduring all the rest worthwhile.

Thus far, the food in Spain hasn't been bad. And it, along with about everything else, is unbelievably cheap, which is why I splurged and bought leather boots and driving gloves. Every meal has cost under $2.

For lunch today, we had paella—a Spanish specialty made with rice, seafood, chicken, sausage, and whatever else might be in the kitchen. Neither of the girls had it before, and both were reluctant to eat the squid tentacles they found scattered through the rice.

The Spanish people seem very friendly and eager to help, especially when it comes to providing directions. But they don't always point the same way to reach the same destination.

Yesterday was Thanksgiving, but I wouldn't have remembered if the girls hadn't mentioned it. They remembered, they said, because they forgot their own Thanksgiving and didn't remember until someone told them. With glasses of red wine we toasted our holidays. Spanish wine is just as good as French, I think. One of them is called Sangre de Toro, bull's blood.

Nov. 29, Barcelona

Saturday was a day of recovery. Friday night, we introduced the girls to sangria at a Flamenco show and then followed with a few other assorted beverages. One of the dancers and I did a bit of flirting, holding each other's gaze for several seconds at a time, both when she was dancing and when she was sitting to the side. She seemed like a fiery wench, with flaring nostrils, dark eyes, and long black hair. I guess I seemed like a tourist, although there doesn't seem to be too many in Barcelona. Anyway, whether the encounter was real or imagined, possibly inspired by the sangria, it added a little excitement.

In the aftermath, the girls didn't leave their hotel room until Saturday evening. Meanwhile, Alessio and I explored the waterfront. That night, we enjoyed an Americanized version of a Spanish Saturday evening. Or maybe it was the other way around.

At any rate, we went to a movie—"M.A.S.H," dubbed in Spanish—and followed that up with a stop at an "Orange Julius" for non-alcoholic refreshments and then a stroll along the Ramblas. It seemed as if all Barcelona was out and half of them did the same thing we did. But most all of them were more formally dressed than we were. The men wore coats and ties, while most of the women wore dresses.

Our seats in the old playhouse, which now serves as a theater, were in the back row of the balcony. It was the first time I ever sat above a chandelier.

We went to Montjuich on Sunday. We reached the mountain by taking a funicular across the harbor. We saw a village, featuring typical examples of Spanish architecture and an old fortress overlooking the city. Then we went to a nearby amusement park. I haven't been on so many rides since I was 12, maybe not even then. I'm sure I had more stamina and probably more sense back then. We staggered away after about two hours of hard riding.

*****

Today, Alessio, Brenda, Sue, and I rented a car for five days and spent the first at Montserrat, a mountain holding a monastery built in the 11th century. We rode a cable car up a steep incline to reach our destination. At the top, we were greeted by a burro. The most striking thing about the place for me was that so many miracles of healing seemed to have occurred there, evidenced by the canes, crutches, and prosthetics left behind by pilgrims.

Alessio is our driver, and it should be an exciting week—if we live. Actually, he seems quite a good driver, and he is a veteran of the auto madness in Rome. "In Rome, you have five cars in three lanes," Alessio said.

Smog in Barcelona was horrible today. And it reached as far as Montserrat, which is about 40 kilometers away.

As I examined Spanish paper money, I idly mentioned that foreign currency doesn't seem like real money to me and perhaps that's why I can spend it so easily. The others said that they feel the same way.

Here's a news flash: Spain's French fries are far better than those in France. The French versions usually are too greasy. In general, the Spanish food seems to be just as good as the French, and there's often more of it. The seafood is great here, and I've been trying all sorts of things, including squid prepared three different ways.

We've learned that the Spanish will hold an election in mid-December to determine if their government will become a democracy. Signs are all over the place, saying such things as: "Your voice is your vote" and "Inform yourself and vote." Then, only a few feet from nearly every sign, you see a soldier with a machine gun, and you wonder if the people really ever will have a voice in their own affairs. Do they even care? For most of them, life wouldn't change one bit with a democracy. But if choosing a democracy will get rid of those ubiquitous soldiers, I'm all for it.

Nov. 30, Barcelona

Today we met a monkey in the market and then had two flat tires within minutes of each other. At first, I didn't think there could be a connection. But then I analyzed the situation: None of us ever had two flat tires in one day before. And none of us ever met a monkey in the market before. So…

My hypothesis didn't exactly meet with enthusiastic approval. But we forward thinkers always have had to deal with ridicule.

The monkey actually was a chimp, dressed in blue jeans and roller skates. He also was wearing a white sweater, as was his owner, or master, or parent, or whatever one calls a person who escorts a skating chimp by the hand through a crowded fruit and vegetable market.

We had the flat tires on the way up the Costa Brava. We didn't get far. The right rear tire flattened on us just outside of Barcelona. The next occurred less than 5 kilometers later, and it was the spare we had used to replace the first flat. The only mechanic in the town of Masnou was having his siesta when we got to the garage. Fortunately, we were near a section of the coast with a small beach, so we waited there and enjoyed a picnic lunch.

My Spanish really is improving. I'm good at asking questions such as "Where is the bathroom?" and "Check, please." Now, all I have to do is learn to understand the answers.

Dec. 5, Paris

Well, here I am again in Paris—at least I think it's Paris. I've been so sick the past 24 hours that I'm not too sure about anything. Yesterday's 13-hour train trip from Barcelona was the major reason for my illness, I think. I sat backward the whole way and I didn't drink anything, both of which likely were major contributors. Also, I ate little during the past 24 hours and managed only three hours of sleep the night before the journey. My stomach still feels as if it's tied in a knot.

I was so weak that Alessio and the girls had to help me off the train. Guzzling down a couple of warm Cokes at the hotel seemed to help a bit, which makes me think that dehydration was a big factor.

By the way, we're at the same hotel that I stayed in before. It's clean, quaint, and quiet. And it has bidets! I'd never seen one before that first night in Paris, and thought it was for soaking tired feet. Turns out, that's not what bidets are intended for, even if they seem to work for that. The manager, who speaks broken English, is laid back with a good sense of humor.

I received much needed comic relief this morning at breakfast from a couple from Michigan. They're been traveling for three months. Their 15-hour train ride from Madrid turned into 30 hours. They had no food with them. Another couple felt sorry for them, though, and gave them two cookies.

The guy thinks he contracted food poisoning from a restaurant in Barcelona. They spent Thanksgiving at McDonald's in Geneva and much of their eating time at Burger Bravo in Madrid. The wife said she's been sick "in every major city in Europe," including Florence and Vienna. They stayed four hours in Brindizi, a town in southern Italy where many tourists catch the boat for Greece. They said that they were scared to death the whole time. Evidently, it's a port city with some rough-looking characters.

Sue and Brenda expressed the same sentiments about their time there. On their way back to Rome, they boarded the train with a guy from Great Britain who had just spent a month in Brindizi. He came back from Greece with no money, and thought he could hitchhike out of the city. After about a week, he realized that no one picks up hitchhikers in southern Italy. He had to get a job to earn money for his train ticket, and he had no place to sleep. He spent his nights playing cards at the police station.

Some of the people whom you meet or hear about over here really make you wonder why they're doing this. On the way down to Nice from Avignon, Alessio and I met a girl from Australia who was traveling frantically about so she could get more than her money's worth out of her Eurail pass. She had twice gone from Brussels to Rome, just to use the pass. She was extremely cynical about her trip, especially about time spent in Spain and Italy. She was more vehement than most, but cynicism does seem to be the rule of the day for those who have been traveling more than a month or so.

Our train out of Barcelona yesterday was just as bad as most people say the transportation in Spain is. Sue and I sat next to the window, where a nearby heat duct on the floor sent up enough hot air to heat most of Alaska. Our pants legs heated up so much that we almost couldn't touch them. The guys next to us in the four-seat section were chain smokers, which put fire on one side and smoke on the other.

The French train was much more comfortable, but we had a couple sitting behind us with a dog that barked at everyone who passed by. The dog wore a sweater and jacket. At least it smelled better than the goat on the bus in rural Spain.

And across the aisle was a woman who took some perfume out of her suitcase, sprayed it, and nearly choked us all to death.

*****

Before we left Barcelona, we went to a disco to celebrate Alessio's birthday. Over here, it seems, men think nothing of dancing alone or together, and there were a lot of them out there on the floor. Neither one of us wanted to do the "when in Rome thing" and join them. We chose to do the "Bump" only with women. As it turned out, I really enjoying bumping with Sue, and I suspect the feeling was mutual. Uh, oh, is something going on here?

Also, we tried to drive to Andorra, a small country on the Spain-France border. But we hit snow at 1,300 meters elevation, and, by the time we were deep into the mountains, it was starting to stay on the road. We spent the night in Puigcerda, a beautiful little border town. After checking into a small hotel, we went back to the car to get our gear and ended up having a snowball fight.

As it turned out, inside wasn't a whole lot warmer than outside. The hotel had no heat. It was the first time in my life I ever put on more clothes to go to bed. Alessio and I shared a room, while the girls took another. After our experience at the disco, I realized that I would have preferred to sleep with Sue, and, in the midst of our snowball fight, she confided that she felt the same. We seem to have established a good relationship. But she also said that Brenda did not want to share with Alessio and she's been noticing some tension between them.

Even for someone as naturally clueless regarding relationships as I, it's obvious that he is attracted to her. But evidently the feeling is not mutual. Brenda is rather shy and, according to both Alessio and Sue, constantly putting herself down. Alessio says he's been trying to bring her out of it, but without much luck. Maybe he's trying too hard.

After a quick visit to Andorra—just to say we did it—the drive back to Barcelona was magnificent.

The clouds were breaking up, and we were above them much of the time. The sky was the deepest blue I've seen in Europe, deeper even than what I saw that day on the beach in Nice, which admittedly might have been wine-enhanced.

Oh, yeah, a neat thing happened in Barcelona during our final night there. We had dinner, as usual, at Los Pergaminos, a restaurant just down the street from our hotel. When we told the owner's son we were leaving the next day, he gave us all ashtrays and shook our hands. Then, another waiter came over and shook hands too.

Ever the adventurer, I decided to order "anguilas" there one night. When delivered in a bowl, the food looked like pasta. Actually, it was a mound of baby eels, eyes and all, cooked in olive oil and seasoned with garlic and red pepper. Sue, Brenda, and Alessio declined my offer to share them.

*****

Sue and I did "share" something else later on, in my hotel room.

Brenda's rejection of Alessio kept us from pairing off as couples for occasional intimate time to get better acquainted.

But after we finished with dinner and strolled around the Ramblas for awhile, we retired to our rooms. Alessio and I had considered sharing a room at the Corello, but rates were so cheap that we opted to get separate accommodations. When I heard a knock at my door about 11 p.m. and opened it to see Sue standing there, I was really glad that we weren't sharing.

"I thought maybe we could talk," she said as she stepped inside. "We don't get much opportunity to do that—just the two of us."

"No, we don't," I replied.

"And since Brenda and I are sharing a room, it's not like you could come to ours and we could have any privacy," said my Canadian cutie with curly brown hair.

"No, I couldn't," I acknowledged.

"Would you if we could have?" she asked.

"Yes, I would have," I said. "And I'm really glad you came."

"Really?" she said softly, avoiding my eyes as she looked around the room. "I'm not so sure. I'm not usually this forward. And now I'm feeling a little embarrassed."

"Please, don't be," I said. "I'm not forward either, especially with girls, and especially since I'm just coming off a divorce."

Yikes! I wasn't sure why, but revealing that seemed to be a gigantic mistake on my part.

Sue's face grew red and she turned back toward the door. "I made a mistake," she said. "You're not ready for this. I'm sorry."

I grabbed her hand and pulled her back. "No you didn't," I said. "I like you, Sue. I really do."

She allowed me to pull her over to the bed, where we sat down together. Then I kissed her.

"Okay, then tell me about it," she said, as I pulled away.

So I did. I told her that I had married much too young—at 24—because it was what I was supposed to do after graduating college, serving in the military and getting my first job. And less than four years later, I added, my wife and I separated, and, for the first time in my life, I felt free to do whatever I wanted.

And what I wanted was go come to Europe, and especially Paris.

"I never gave any thought to meeting people like you and Brenda and Alessio, who were doing the same thing I was, and having an adventure together," I said.

"So… I'm just part of an adventure you're having?" Sue said with a sly smile.

Before I could protest, she put her hand over my mouth. "That's okay, Robert," she said. "You're part of my adventure too."

Then she began to unbutton my shirt and we shared an adventure together.

Not having been intimate with a woman besides my wife for more than four years made it difficult, but not "hard" for me, if you know what I mean. But Sue helped me with that.

In full disclosure and respect for the truth: That conversation between Sue and me might not have been exactly as I transcribed it. I mean, my mind was on other things than being a good reporter. But I think it's reasonably accurate. And the talking part of our encounter ended exactly as I described it.

Dec. 6, Paris

When we left a restaurant in the Latin Quarter tonight, we came face to face with a guy breathing fire! Talk about dragon mouth!

We dodged the flames and went on our way.

Alessio told me that he thinks Brenda is cool toward him because she likes me very much. It's something I had noticed too, but was reluctant to mention. I like her too, but Sue is the one who knocked on my hotel door in Barcelona—and I'm glad she was.

And while I'm thinking about women—which I often do—and returning to Barcelona for a moment, Alessio and I got in a taxi after returning the rental car. Our cab pulled up next to another cab carrying a beautiful young woman. She turned toward me. After that, I'm not certain of the exact sequence of events before we both smiled broadly as our taxis separated and vanished into the night.

Then there was that French woman who seemed to undress me with her eyes as we passed each other one day on the Pont Neuf. God, I love European women! And I'm more than okay with Canadians too!

Dec. 9, Paris

The last few days have been rather uneventful, except I have discovered Sue is more serious about me than I am about her. She gave me a book entitled "Impressionism" and signed it "Paris, 1976, Love, Sue." Of course that in itself is simply a generous gesture from one friend to another. But then throw in the fact that she often touches me as we talk and she takes my hand as we walk, which—I won't deny—I enjoy too. We kissed tonight—and ditto on the mutual enjoyment.

But now I'm thinking that she considers me a much more important part of her European experience than I do her in relation to mine. Yes, I like her. Yes, I'm physically attracted to her. But… well, I don't want to start a serious relationship so soon after my divorce. I want to have an adventure. At the same time, I guess that I feel like a heel. I never intended to deceive her. And she's the one who knocked on my door.

Last night, she said she was so afraid "something like this wasn't going to happen." A romantic encounter, I suspect, is what she means by "this." From there, the conversation got even more confusing—and disturbing—at least for me. There really is physical chemistry there between us, but I meant it when I said—or tried to say before she stopped me—that she was a part of my European adventure. I mean, she's from western Canada and I'm from Florida by way of Missouri, and forming a long-term relationship is the last thing on my mind, even after we shared our last night together in Barcelona.

But when it comes to women, I am painfully naive, as well as shy, despite being married for more than three years. Or maybe it's because I was married.

No, I think that I've always been that way, both naïve and shy. I realize that guys are supposed to be the aggressor, the pursuer, but I'm just not that way, and never have been. Possibly it's because I have low self-esteem. Also, it seems to me that I've always been years behind my peers in terms of important milestones of growing up. I didn't get my driver's license until I was 18. I had only one date in high school, and it was coerced by friends who thought I should go to prom. In a way, maybe this European adventure is for me what life after high school or college is for more "normal" people. Paging Dr. Freud!

We leave for London tomorrow. Alessio will be staying with friends.

Maybe I'm going to have to avoid spending too much time with the girls, especially Sue, while there. I don't want to hurt her, but I don't want to mislead her either. For me, this really is all about having an adventure, and not about jumping into another relationship so quickly after a failed marriage.

*****

With the girls and Alessio, I made a return visit to the Louvre today. I took photos of Japanese tourists taking photos of the Venus de Milo. Containing the Mona Lisa and so many other renowned works of art, the Louvre is a wonderful place, and I could wander around there for hours. I also thoroughly enjoyed the Rodin Museum.

But the Jeu de Paume, housing works of Monet, Degas, Van Gogh, and other impressionists, remains my favorite. This small-town boy from Missouri actually got to see the original of the Monet sailboats print that he had hanging on a barracks wall when he was in the Army! To stand among and admire so many works of art that I'd seen and read about in books all in one place was… well, I don't know the word for it.

Still, I'm glad I haven't spent too much of my time in Europe in museums. The joy of travel, I've found, is more often discovered outside the walls than in. The cities and their people are what are worth coming to see, as well as meeting others who are doing the same thing.

Jerry and Alice are from Seattle. He has a PhD in sociology, and she taught nursing for awhile. They've been traveling for about three months. Their best stories are about the trains in Italy. At the train station in Florence, they tried to find out how much it would cost to travel from Florence to Munich and on to Paris. They were told they would have to go to Munich to find out how much it costs to go to Paris.

Two nights ago, we went to an Algerian restaurant with them for a dinner of couscous, a grain dish covered with meat, vegetables, and sauce. The sauce was a bit on the hot side. Now I know where that guy breathing fire must have dined the other night.

I took everyone to a French restaurant—Chez Alexandre—last night. I had been there twice the first time around. The waiters remembered me, and they gave us a free bottle of wine.

The first time I went there, entertainment was provided by a guy playing a guitar and singing Spanish words that bore absolutely no relation to one another. He was yelling things like "Hombre!" and "Arriba!" and Tequila!" At least the guy last night knew some Spanish songs. Jerry asked him if he knew any Woody Guthrie. The closest he came was "Yankee Doodle."

Let's see, in Paris I've been to Greek, Italian, Chinese, and Algerian restaurants, as well as a couple of

French ones. French food is good all right, but I've enjoyed the other kinds more.

Spanish seafood still gets the highest rating, squids and all. Of course, the most memorable was the "Anguilas Bilbao style," that bowl of about a thousand tiny eels—eyes and all—floating in a clear sauce with garlic and red pepper.

Dec. 10, London

We saw "A Chorus Line" tonight. I'm hoping it is only the first of many plays I'll see in London. Our seats were on the top row in back, but still quite good. And they cost just $4 each. Try to do that in New York City.

Tomorrow night, we going to see "No Sex, Please, We're British." How great it must be to live in a city where you can see so many good plays so cheaply.

When we arrived in London today, the sky was a crisp blue, without a cloud in it. And, can you believe it, the humidity was very low. Even though the temperature was about 36 degrees Fahrenheit, it was the most comfortable I've been outside since Nice.

It didn't take long to see my first queue. The girls told me the British queue for everything, even when there are only two people. And they're right. We queued at the bus stop, the bank, the theatre, etc. It's such a welcome, orderly relief from France and Spain where people just push and shove to get what they want.

Orderliness is reflected in signs too. And, boy, do the British love signs. They're everywhere. A sign on the subway gives a list of six instructions to follow if you find a lost or unattended parcel, the first of which is not to touch.

There are signs on the public restrooms saying where the next closest facilities are if the one you're at happens to be closed. There are signs in our hotel saying do not block the hallway. There are signs on buildings saying "Barkers Prohibited." Does that mean no dogs allowed?

There are signs on street posts warning it is illegal for your dog to "Foul the Pavement." There are signs at the intersections saying which way to look before crossing.

It's really been strange coming to a place where English is spoken. I'm still taken aback to hear it everywhere. I guess the novelty will fade in a day or two.

It's also a jolt to hear small children speak with a proper British accent.

As a person who loves language, I'm eager to hear the many different figures of speech there must be over here. The best so far is, "What time do you want to be knocked up in the morning?"

Oh, yeah, their exit signs say "Way Out." And the signs on fast food restaurants say, "Take Away" instead of "Take Out."

Our bed and breakfast hotel is just around the corner from Dickens' home, and it's close by the British Museum and part of the University of London.

Dec. 12, London

Wouldn't' you know it? My only weekend in London and the **Sunday Times** isn't published because of a strike.

Sign of the day: "Polite Notice. Don't Park Your Car Outside the Hotel."

We were sitting in front of the gas fire tonight in the girls' room, after a long day of walking through Hyde Park and Kensington Gardens. Sue evidently got a bit too close, for the crepe soles of her shoes melted and stuck to the carpet.

It's still disconcerting to see a car go by you and see what appears to be a small child or dog driving. I keep forgetting the steering wheel is on the right instead of the left over here.

We went to see "No Sex, Please" last night and did as the British do and took some chocolate or "sweets," as they call them.

The weather finally looked as if it belonged here today, cold, cloudy, and damp, and there was little going on in Hyde Park. The few speakers there didn't have much to say, but they used a lot of words to do it. The best speech was an attack on Arabs, "the most primitive people." By "best" I mean coherent. It was also quite vehement and biting. Most of the speakers expound on political issues.

Alessio, by the way, is often thought to be Arab—by Arabs. I guess his black, curly hair and mustache are the reasons. In France and Spain, Arab men often came running and yelling up to him as if he were a long, lost brother. He hated that!

*****

I've been sort of melancholy the past few days, and Sue asked me about it tonight. She said it sounds as if I've had "an overdose of people." And, I think that's exactly what it is. I've never spent such a long time in major cities. And, wherever I've ever lived or traveled before, I've always been able to get away, to fish, to walk, to be alone for awhile. It's not like that now.

I still feel good physically and mentally. The trip has been everything I expected and more. It has been a great adventure, one that I had the courage to take entirely on my own, except for Arthur Frommer's book. But I feel a depression of the spirit and a great understanding of the verse on the poster that my ex-wife gave me just after we were married: "I live not in myself, but I become a part of that around me. And to me high mountains are a feeling. And the hum of human cities, torture."

The aimlessness of the days might be a part of it too, out on the streets from morning to evening without a goal or objective in mind or anything to look forward to. Add a dash of cold weather, and people who don't really stimulate you, and you have reason for melancholy.

But, more than anything, I'm sure it's being in cities for so long, living with crowds and traffic and noise. That's not how I want to spend my life. And, right now, I think it's time to leave.

Sue told me that Canada has lots of wild places, with beautiful scenery and good fishing, and she would love to show them to me.

"But just you and me," she added. "No Brenda and no Alessio."

"Sounds good to me," I said.

She smiled at my response, but her brown eyes reflected doubt.

"Hey, I mean it," I said, as I took her hand. "I'd love to see Canada with you as my tour guide."

But did I mean it? Sure I'd like to experience the great outdoors of Canada. And I do like Sue. Still… My gut tells me that she wants something that I'm just not ready to give in terms of a relationship.

I guess that we'll just have to see how this plays out. Both here in London and when we return to our respective countries.

And in thinking about that, I realized something pretty incredible. I'll be going back to the U.S. with absolutely no prospects, no job, no nothing except the fishing gear and clothes stored at my parents' house in Missouri and my MGB in their garage. That's a little scary, of course. But this trip has given me supreme confidence in just living life as it comes and then making the best of opportunities as they present themselves.

So, yes, I am feeling a little melancholy. But I've also just discovered that—with no prospects—yet another great adventure awaits me back in Missouri or more likely Florida, where I was living as a gainfully employed and happily married man what seems like a century ago. And, who knows, maybe I will go explore Canada with Sue as my tour guide.

Dec. 13, London

We nearly lingered too long in an Italian restaurant tonight and had to hurry to get to the theater in time. As we emerged from the subway station nearest the theatre, we were engulfed by crowds of people lining both sides of the street. We fought our way to an intersection, wondering aloud what all the fuss was about.

A young man with long hair pushed his way clear near us, heard us talking, and said in a wonderfully British manner, "Oh, the silly, old queen is coming." He then hurried on his way, probably rushing to a play too.

We never did see "the silly old queen." But we did see "Jesus Christ Superstar." It was really a treat for me to hear the parents behind us explaining the play—between acts—to their children. My parents never were that way, and it's taken a while for me to learn life can be different, and better, than what I experienced. Of course, the flip side of that is that it could be worse.

I don't regret having to learn so much on my own—including the facts of life. But there is more to the parent-child relationship than imparting knowledge, something a self-taught person misses. Parent and child can share love, affection, and respect, as well as knowledge. I didn't get much of that, although I was well cared for in a material way.

Dec. 14, London

We saw "Equus" tonight. It's a play about a psychiatrist who questions the validity of his own existence, while treating a young man who literally worshipped horses, before inexplicably blinding six of them. The doctor seems almost to envy the passion the young man has experienced, even though that passion is viewed as an illness. The doctor's own world, evidently, is void of feeling.

On the way back to the hotel, Sue told us how "strange" the people usually are who work in hospital psychiatric wards. She said that one doctor married two of his patients. One at a time, of course.

A nurse in one ward committed suicide. The staff then deliberated for several days about whether they should tell her patients. They finally told them and, of course, all the patients blamed themselves.

On a more cheery note, there's the sign of the day: "Orienteering: Cunning Running."

Dec. 15, London

Signs of the day in order of sighting:

1. Posted on a large, otherwise blank wall: "Notice: Bill stickers will be prosecuted."

2. Post on a wall opposite Trafalgar Square: "London School for Nonviolence in the Crypt."

3. Sign carried by a young man as he passed Palace Theater: "I choked Linda Lovelace." Alessio and I immediately laughed, while the girls were puzzled by our response. Explaining the double meaning was a little embarrassing.

We saw Somerset Maugham's "The Circle" this afternoon. Then we saw "Side by Side by Sondheim" tonight. So did Julie Andrews. We didn't sit together.

With husband Blake Edwards, Julie drew as big a crowd outside the theater as "the silly old queen."

On the way to the theatre this evening, we passed Trafalgar Square, where a large Christmas tree had been erected and children were singing carols, creating a scene right out of Dickens.

And that reminds me: We did a bit of Christmas shopping in Harrods. Yikes! What a store! I'd never seen anything like it in terms of size, variety, and luxury items of every description.

Before we wandered our separate ways to buy gifts, we all sat down at a counter and inhaled rich and chocolaty milkshakes. They were wonderful! Aside from cheese, a little milk in café au lait, and some hot chocolate at a little café in the mountains of Spain, that was the first dairy we'd had in weeks.

Deciding to go all out, I bought a Pierre Cardin silk scarf for my sister and an expensive French perfume, Joy, for my mother.

After a fish and chips dinner tonight, we got together in a pub with Terry and Alice for one last drink. And, as I sit here tonight in my bed and breakfast room, overlooking a foggy London street, it's almost impossible to fathom that tomorrow night I'll be back in small-town America, at my parents' house in Flat River, Missouri.

Since she's sharing a room with Brenda, Sue stopped by mine so we could say our goodbyes in private. In the morning, we won't be going to the airport at the same time, since she and Brenda are on a much later flight than mine.

I do like her. I will miss her. I told her so, and she said the same to me. She also cried a little after we kissed and hugged and promised to stay in touch.

She gave me her address, and I gave her mine—or rather my parents'. After all, I'm a vagabond at the moment.

"Please come to Canada," she said with a smile. "I'll show you a good time. I promise."

She was intentionally making a joke, trying to lighten the moment, and we both laughed, or pretended to anyway. But still I was profoundly sad, and clearly she was too. We both remembered that wonderful night together in Barcelona.

"I'd love to. Really," I said, as I pulled her back to me for one last kiss.

But truthfully, that probably was the last time we'd ever see each other.

Yet my plans for the future don't extend past spending the holidays with my family in Missouri and then probably heading back down to Florida for awhile.

I'm thinking that this trip to Europe might be just the first part of my Great Adventure. So… who knows?

Part II:
Home for the Holidays

Dec. 18, Flat River, Mo.

Wow, culture shock! I've gone from one of the world's most cosmopolitan cities to small-town U.S.A.

But, I must admit, it's nice to be home at Christmas for the first time in quite a few years. Sitting here by the artificial Christmas tree makes me nostalgic and brings back pleasant memories of my childhood.

At least this plastic tree is green! Back in the early 60s, we had a god-awful aluminum tree sitting in front of the picture window, illuminated by a revolving color wheel. Even then, I thought it was hideous, especially since it replaced our traditional cut tree, a balsam fir. I loved it for the smell as much as for its appearance.

But Mom said the falling needles "make too much of a mess" so she was all in for the aluminum atrocity.

Stockings that I helped design when I was 10 hang on the mantle of the electric fireplace on the other side of the living room. Back then, we had a real fireplace, along with a real tree.

The pattern that Mom used for the red, oversized felt stockings didn't include a reindeer, so I drew one!

And as the oldest, I got to pick out which of the three glitter trims that I preferred. I took gold, my sister red, and my brother was stuck with green.

And just the year before about this time, I discovered that Santa Claus wasn't real when I chased a bouncing ball into my parents' room and under the their bed—where I found a box containing what appeared to be a bicycle. I wanted to believe that the bike would be given to me as a present from them, while Santa would bring something else. But in my heart, I knew that wouldn't be the case. I was right.

I didn't say anything, although I'm not sure why. Still, I'm glad I kept my mouth shut. My brother was just a year old, so it wouldn't have mattered for him. But my sister was 5, and I guess that I didn't want to spoil the magic for her.

Honestly, I'm not feeling much magic these days. I'm more on the crabby side, so I'm going to whine a little.

Just as they have for years, Mom and Dad still complain about the dog next door barking early every morning, without doing anything about it. Mom still says "don't" when she should say "doesn't." Yikes! That's like fingernails scraping a chalkboard for me.

As I'm writing, my Dad just asked me a question. Instead of giving him a brief answer, as I usually do, I decided to go into an explanation.

Things haven't changed. He didn't pay attention to a word. And Craig says he (my father) tells my mother I never talk to him. I guess that's right, because he doesn't listen.

Actually, neither one of them does—except when Mom is in the kitchen and others are having a conversation in the living room. Then she hears everything.

Of course, there was juicy gossip awaiting my arrival. The local conservation agent found a man and woman in a parked car, passed out from carbon monoxide. Mom said he revived them by mouth-to-mouth, and they were then taken to the hospital.

"She weighed about 350 pounds and didn't have any clothes on," Mom said. "He had his pants on, but they were pulled down."

The man, it seems, had told his wife he was coming down here (from St. Louis) to go deer hunting. Or maybe it was "dear hunting."

My friend Eric, who owns a hardware store, is sharing his house with Kathy, who tried to commit suicide about two months ago. He's afraid to tell her to move out, he said, because "her father is a hit man." Yeah, that would give me pause as well.

Bill is there too. He was contemplating suicide, Eric said, because of his recent divorce. He insists he never will get over the grief caused by the loss of his children. He is on some sort of medication.

For many people around here it seems, it's not "such a wonderful life."

Dec. 22, Flat River

I've been feeling depressed for the past couple of days. Part of it is my eagerness to return to Florida and part of it is Flat River in general. But mostly, I think, it stems from meeting a girl named Kelly.

I met her at Eric's Christmas party Sunday night, and went home with her afterward. She's a beautiful girl who's very lonely, I think. She's been in this area only since September, and already she's got quite a reputation. Since I went home with her, Eric has delighted in putting her down and talking about how "easy" she is.

For him, girls are nothing but conquests to be added to his list. As I think about it, I've known quite a few guys who were that way, going all the way back to high school.

Essentially, Eric and Kelly are doing the same thing, but for vastly different reasons. His superficiality is part of the reason for my depression, as his dismissal of another human being's search for happiness. I suspect that, around here, he is the rule rather than the exception.

Kelly is originally from here. She got married a week after she was graduated from high school.

She was three months' pregnant at the time. She got pregnant to get married and got married to escape a step-father she hated.

The child died in its sleep. It was all right one night, dead the next morning. She then had a miscarriage, and later a divorce. She next married a man 16 years older than she.

Until September, she was living in Pennsylvania with him. Some months before that, she discovered he was seeing another woman. They talked about it, and he, evidently, led her to believe they could work things out when she returned from visiting her mother and sister here. After she arrived, he called her and told her not to bother returning. He then sent her car and clothes down to her. While they were married, she had her tubes tied, since he already had six children.

So… now she's 26 and has nothing but a fur coat, a Datsun 240Z, and a lot of bad memories. She was never unfaithful to her husband and now, I suspect, she's making up for that. She has no one to talk to, she said, and she can't bear being alone. She's giving sex—the way I see it—for companionship. At the same time, she's built a shell around her to avoid getting hurt again.

*****

My sister wanted to know what to get me for Christmas. "A teapot," I said.

"For what?" my mother asked.

A Pizza Hut opened in a nearby town a few weeks ago. The first week, a woman put her car through one of the walls. Maybe she thought it was a drive-thru restaurant.

Eric wants me to play Santa Claus downtown for the Chamber of Commerce. Betty, who owns an optical business with her husband, said she would make it worth my while.

Betty nearly raped me under the Christmas tree at Eric's party—after her husband had gone home. She's another lonely one. She's 34, with three children and, I think, totally bored with her life.

There's also Kathy, who's found security with Eric, and won't move out of his house no matter how shabbily he treats her. He took another girl to bed with him Friday night, and Kathy, wearing his college ring, slept on the couch.

It's really a sad, depressing scene around here sometimes.

Dec. 23, *Flat River*

I have a lot more time to write here than I did in Europe. Too much time.

Here's the big news of the day, as reported by my mother, who, after all these years, still goes to the supermarket almost every day:

A little boy was running up and down the aisles, pushing a shopping cart in front of him. His sister was in the cart. An old man stepped into their path and was sent flying.

I had lunch with Kelly yesterday, and we talked some more. Her first marriage was used to get away from home. Her second was to a man who took her places and spent money on her. "Infatuation," she called it. Her next, if there is one, she said, "will be for love."

I'm pretty certain that she will marry again. Me? I'm not so certain. Right now, I don't have a clue what I want, and I'm okay with that. Getting on that plane alone to go to Europe, with no plans for when I got there and no plans for when I returned, has blessed me with a self-confidence that I didn't know I was capable of. That trip worked out great. And so will whatever the future brings. Anyway, life is what happens to you while you're making plans.

Kelly's cousin, Jim, a friend of my brother, told me tonight that Kelly is searching for love and security. That's good insight for someone only 20 years old. He also said that she likes me because I'm not like "the rest of the guys around here."

*****

I've always avoided attaching too much importance to material possessions. That was one of the areas of conflict for my ex-wife and me. For her, appearance was paramount. She wanted not only for us to be successful but to look it. She used to call me "ol' flannel shirt and blue jeans."

But I never stopped to think about possible reasons for my aversion. Tonight, I was hit over the head with a big reason: My mother.

My family has two sets of encyclopedias. One of them is fairly new. The other is more than 20 years old. I suggested to mother that the old set should be given to a library or some other appropriate place. She immediately became angry. She said she used the older set "to look things up that aren't in the other books." And she said she was saving the set for my niece. By the time she can read, those books will be almost 30 years old.

By the way, she has placed the books backward, from Z to A, on the shelves.

Mom also saves paper bags, buttons, bows, scraps of material, anything and everything. She has three closets full of clothing, and told my father she wants clothes for Christmas because she doesn't have anything to wear.

I cleaned out table drawers in the living room the other day—without her knowing it—and threw away more than 20 phone books, some of them 15 years old. And there were doubles and triples of some.

When I returned from Europe, I threw away a lot of the literature that I had collected about the places I might want to visit. The next day, I noticed several of the pamphlets and brochures on her dresser.

This place is a pack rat's paradise. And, I guess, it also provides security. To acquire and acquire, and never throw anything away, makes the nest seem safer, more comfortable. It drives me crazy sometimes.

But I also can understand it, and I guess I should be a little more tolerant. Throughout my childhood we moved a lot. I can remember living in six different houses before we settled here in 1964, when I was a junior in high school. I hated moving so often and going to so many different schools. And although I'd never thought about it before, I'd bet that Mom did too. I am certain that she doesn't like change; she wants things to be the way that they always were, the way that she's comfortable with. She's had 13 years to get comfortable here, and a big part of that is never throwing anything away.

Jan. 1, 1977, Flat River

I spent New Year's Eve with Middle America.

First, Kelly and I went to a party at her friend Judy's house. Judy looked as if she just stepped out of a time warp. I hadn't seen so much teased hair since high school. Her husband wore a yellow leisure suit, and made ice cubes in the shape of naked women.

He made a big production out of coming into the kitchen, where we were sitting, to "get some ice." He sucked on the cubes and made a few appropriate remarks so everyone would know how clever he is.

Later, we all went to a dance at the National Guard Armory. One girl, Debbie, was drunk before we left the house. Kelly said it happens all the time. Debbie is always alone, always drunk.

Kelly also said she saw a lot of the "Chateau regulars" at the dance. Chateau is a local hangout and I went there a couple of times with Eric before I left for Europe. Kelly told me that she goes there at least three times a week, and, evidently, many others do too. Kelly said she can't bear to stay at home.

When she is home, she makes a concerted effort to sleep as much as possible. That's what's she will be doing this weekend. I left her house at noon today, and she still was dead to the world.

Life seems to be so much of a burden for the people around here. Perhaps it's that way everywhere, but it took me getting close to people here to find that out.

Pill popping is a way of life, a necessity for getting through the day. Eric provides some for friends, as well as taking them himself. I don't know where he gets them. Kathy has to take them to keep from being in deep depression. Bill, the principal, is taking some to help ease the pain of his divorce.

Melinda takes them too. She's 19 and divorced. Her ex-husband broke her jaw while they were married and knocked out some of her teeth with a hammer. Melinda talks as if she gets by on less than 10 hours of sleep a week. She had a physical collapse the other day, and was taken home from work. But she couldn't sleep because "I'm too hyper."

Kipper is 28, twice married, with three boys. I don't' see how she makes it on the money she gets from singing in the band at the Chateau.

What a depressing scene this place can be. Yet it's comfortable. I could fit in, I guess. People want me to stay too. But I can't. Life means too much to me to spend it here—at least the way they live it. I'd rather have insecurity, even failure, as I explore my options and see the world than live in the security of so tedious a place. No one here is excited about life or living. They just go through the motions.

Jan. 9, Flat River

More snow! Will I ever be able to leave for Florida?

It's too bad there are no ski slopes around here. The snow—about 10 inches—is dry and powdery because the temperature is so cold, perfect for skiing. This kind of snow also glitters and sparkles in the light. If the sun ever comes out, the whole place will look as if it's made of crystal. As Craig and I were walking down the street tonight, the street lights made the roads look like beds of diamonds. And the parked cars looked like giant fish with glistening scales.

*****

I squeezed a squirt bottle of ketchup last night, and the top popped off. Ketchup covered me, the table, chair, wall, and, oh yeah, my French fries.

Mom, my favorite pack rat, has five bottles of the same kind of shampoo in the bathroom closet, with varying amounts in them. I gotta get out of this place!

Kathy asked me "what I see" in Kelly the other night at the Chateau. I told her I don't judge people by what other people say. I also told her Kelly has had a lot of problems lately, just as we all have, and we do things to cope, to get by, things we might not do under less trying times.

I hope that the message hit home and Kathy thought of her own depression and the overdose of pills she took. Maybe it did. She and Kelly spent the rest of the evening writing notes to one another. Kelly later told me Kathy wanted to be friends with her.

Kelly keeps saying she doesn't care what other people think, and I think that's probably true. I just hope that shell she's building to keep people out doesn't trap her in. The world's too lonely a place to live like that.

Look who's talking. I started developing one when I was 9 or 10 because of fear of my father. Until I wrote an article about child abuse two years ago, I hadn't even realized that was what happened to me.

Eric told me last night he "doesn't need anyone." It's really hard for him to admit he cares for anyone. So he subordinates his feelings, and lists and rates his conquests. He's afraid he won't reach 50. That's 50 conquests, not 50 years of age.

Last night, he told me he has "animal magnetism." I didn't have the heart to tell him one of the Chateau's waitresses called him "the short, bald guy with the pointed nose."

Jan. 14, Flat River

Finally the roads are clear of snow and ice and I'm heading for Florida tomorrow morning. I don't know what awaits me there, but I'm not worried about it. In fact, I'm looking forward to it. Yes, I'll have to make enough money to live on, but something will turn up. Maybe I'll stop by the newspaper where I used to work as a features writer to say hello to friends and see what's going on there.

Kelly and I said our goodbyes over dinner tonight. We both knew our relationship was only temporary. But she was lonely and so was I, and we made the best of it. I hope she finds love and security with someone, but it won't be me.

Eric asked me to be his business partner. Of course, I declined. I don't know much, but I know retail is not for me. When I made the mistake of telling my father about the offer and my refusal, he exploded with anger. Wow. Yes, I know he has a violent temper. I saw it especially when I was a kid. But this seemed to be out of nowhere.

"I never got to do what I wanted to," he yelled. "Why should you?"

And that goes a long, long way in explaining why my father is a depressed alcoholic, who explodes with rage from time to time.

Florida, here I come.

Part III:
Mono and Mayhem

April 23, Tallahassee, Fla.

I wish I hadn't stayed away from this journal for so long—more than three months! I've got lots of catching up to do.

I arrived in Tallahassee on Jan. 16 and got sick that evening, while having dinner with my friends, the Mayfields, at their house. In addition to feeling feverish and having a sore throat, my neck started to swell. They thought it might be the mumps. Doctor at the emergency room diagnosed my illness as strep throat and gave me a prescription for Ampicillin, an antibiotic.

But it wasn't strep, a fact that became painfully obvious when I finished the prescription and suddenly started breaking out in a rash from my feet to my head. I looked like I had rubbed myself down with poison ivy leaves.

That's a side effect of taking a Penicillin-based drug while you have mononucleosis. That's right. At age 28, I had mono.

After he gave me a steroid shot in the butt to deal with the rash, the doctor apologized for the misdiagnosis and said, "You're a little old to be getting mono, don't you think?"

He was correct, of course. And there you have it again. That's another example of me being years behind my peers.

I had been sleeping on the Mayfields' couch for a week. But that wasn't going to be sufficient for the several weeks of bed rest required to recover from mono. So they rented a bed for me and put it in their living room.

When I was recently separated from Lois and still working at the newspaper, I met Grace Mayfield in an evening writing class. We quickly became friends and, when she realized that I was going through a tough time, she, her husband, Doug, and their four teenage daughters just sort of adopted me, kindly including me in activities so I wouldn't be alone.

Actually, the daughters, Karen (17), Linda Jane (15), and the identical twins Rachel and Rebecca (13) are Grace's daughters from a previous marriage. She and Doug, who's 12 years younger than she and about my age, have been married only at short time. They met at Florida State, where's she's an administrator.

All the girls are strikingly beautiful.

So… through February, I had the absolute best of care from my good friends, and, of course, we became even closer. The only negative was that Doug, who's in pharmacy school, insisted I eat liver (for the iron, I think) to help with my recovery.

Staying with the Mayfields for a month was one of the best things that ever happened to me. There's a lot of love in that family, and now I'm a part of it. I also feel closer and more accepting of my own family now. Of course, that's when they're about a thousand miles away. We'll just have to see how it plays out when we're together again.

Grace told me this week that I've opened up so much and become a much more vocal person. I was sensitive before, she said, but now I'm telling people how I feel.

That's really interesting, considering that I didn't even know I was doing it most of the time. I'm guessing that's about instinctive survival behavior, acquired while living with six people who are *not* afraid to tell you how they feel.

*****

And what's a writer to do after an experience like that? He writes about it, of course. And that's what I did. I penned a column entitled "Years Behind My Peers" for the **Tallahassee Democrat** newspaper.

That's right. I went back to work at the paper as a features writer and weekly columnist. I hadn't intended to, when I stopped by to see friends there in early March. But management had changed, and I was offered $20 more a week. And I need the money, both to repay the Mayfields for their generosity and get a place of my own. If this is not the right thing to do, I'll know it soon enough, I guess. But until then, I have income.

Although management is new, I'm certain the editors heard about what I did, just before I left the first time. To reach an outside phone line at the paper, you have to dial "1." Sometimes it works, and other times you get an ear-piercing buzz that lots of people complained about.

When I was feeling especially fragile and frazzled one afternoon because of my impending divorce, that buzz in the ear pushed me over the edge. I picked up the telephone and hurled it against the wall, shattering it into dozens, or perhaps hundreds, of pieces. I don't know for sure because I didn't stop to examine the carnage.

The newsroom suddenly became mortuary silent, as I calmly pushed my chair under the desk and walked out the door. The next day, I had a new phone and no one ever said a word to me about the incident.

But I'm sure a few words were spoken about it when I wasn't around, including to the new editors. Still, they hired me.

And I've rented a basement apartment in an old two-story house owned by a sweet little lady named

Mrs. Gunn. She often talks about how pretty the yard used to be and how tirelessly her late husband worked to make it that way.

"If he hadn't worked so hard, he might be here now to enjoy it with me," she told me.

*****

It looks as if Rachel might be a Hollywood star. She and Rebecca tried out for extra and bit parts in a movie, **Hank**, to be partially filmed in Tallahassee. A couple of thousand other people went too. Rachel really didn't want to go.

Michael Musto, the executive producer, picked Rachel out of the crowd, and immediately fell in love with her. He said he's going to take her to Hollywood. He said, "I hate to think what the other producers are going to do when they see her."

It looked for awhile as if I might go with her, as a chaperone, for the four to seven weeks of filming. But Musto recently said he wants her to live with his wife, Dorothy. Musto also is talking about Rachel, and possibly even the family, living out there permanently in a year or two.

Workshops for the movie are being held at the Ramada Inn. Musto always singles out Rachel for special attention, and he has told the group that, so far, she is the only one who definitely will be going to California. Grace said employees at the Ramada know who Rachel is. The family ate out there the other night before a workshop and was told the check "has been taken care of."

Cookies were provided during a break one night. Musto asked Rachel how she liked them. Realizing the power she now possesses, Rachel said that she prefers doughnuts. The next night, there were doughnuts.

Grace said that Rachel always thought about a film career, but was afraid to mention it "because it might make it seem less serious." Right now, it looks as if she might be one of those few who really do have their dreams come true.

Meanwhile, I'm more than twice as old as Rachel and still don't know what my dream is. Maybe it's to write books, but… at this point, who knows?

So far, she's taken the attention paid her very well. She certainly doesn't have a big head. It's as if this whole thing was an eventuality she was waiting for, albeit subconsciously.

Karen, who will be 18 on Tuesday, is talking about moving into an apartment with her friend, Nelda. For some reason, Karen, who studied ballet in New York City, thinks she will be magically transformed into an adult at age 18. Then again, what kid doesn't?

For years, when I was married and working, I thought I was an adult. Now, I seriously have my doubts.

Rebecca is an understudy in the opera **Ballad of Baby Doe**. She also might be an extra in **Hank**. Musto has been supportive of her too, Grace said. That's one of the reasons she likes him.

Linda Jane, my favorite of the four, raises Holy Hell when there is talk of going to California. I can't say I blame her. At her age, I would have done the same thing. In fact, I did, attending three different high schools, an experience I wouldn't wish on any adolescent.

I'm not sure why she is my favorite. It's certainly nothing sexual. More likely, I think it's that we seem to be kindred spirits, with similar tastes and opinions.

Needless to say, Grace is reveling in this pandemonium, although, at times, the pace even becomes a bit much for her. The happiness of this family life is so radically different from what she had growing up and in her first marriage.

She has survived an unloving mother who sent her away to boarding school and a homicidal teacher in Connecticut who left her for dead at age 7 or 8. He took her and two other girls to a rural location, sexually abused them, and left them for dead. One did die. Another later committed suicide. Grace attempted it, before extensive counseling helped restore her will to live.

She followed that up with a mentally ill husband whose actions were totally unpredictable. She once came home and discovered he had sawed all the legs off the dining room table. He also hung presents from the ceiling at Christmas and tied down all the chairs. When Linda Jane was in first grade, he taught her to sing the China national anthem. Finally, when Grace genuinely began to fear for the safety of her daughters, she found the courage to break free from their marriage.

Now she has Doug, one of the most sensitive men I've ever known. They seem perfect for each other.

*****

Things are going well for me. My writing is improving, and I've been asked by Dr. John Lee, a time management expert, to help him write a book. He liked the feature article that I wrote about him and what he does to help companies improve their efficiency.

He's going to pay me $1,500 and give me use of his vacation home on Lake Ellen until Sept. 1.

On my way down here from Flat River, I finally realized the perfect vehicle for a novel. The mono postponed my starting it. But soon I will begin work on **Too Dark to See the Light**.

I'm lonely for close companionship. Ironically, I seem to have more friends than ever before. It's a pleasing paradox, and, I know, someone special will come along.

April 25, Tallahassee

Rebecca said yesterday that she is against the Equal Rights Amendment because it would mean homosexuals could get married. With two men, she said, "there would be no one to do the dishes."

I'm not sure that would be a consequence of passage of the ERA. But if it were, I'd be okay with that. I'm a live and let live kind of guy.

What I hadn't realized though is that having a wife means you never have to do the dishes. I sure wish I'd known about that during my marriage.

May 4, Tallahassee

I finally met Michael Musto tonight. He's a small man with dark hair and maybe 60 years old. He told me he co-produced **Robert Montgomery Presents** for television 25 years ago. He also said he wrote the famous "Who's on First?" sketch for Abbott and Costello.

He plans to buy a Cadillac to drive his cocker spaniel, Pepper, back to Hollywood. Pepper didn't enjoy the 16-hour flight to Florida.

Grace and I talked for more than an hour as we waited for Rachel at the Ramada Inn. Rachel might be going to California with Musto in a couple of weeks. Grace said she cried Monday night and she would be miserable, even for a short time, without one of her daughters. But she never would prevent Rachel from going.

I told Grace about Sunny Sullivan, a girl who came into my life recently. She's a stained glass artist from California and has opened a gallery/art store in downtown Tallahassee, displaying and selling works of local artists on consignment.

Sunny is very special. "Special" is a word I picked up from Grace. And life in general is special because of her, Doug, and the girls.

Sunny, a red-head, and I were stranded together Sunday night when my car got stuck in the sand down on the coast. We didn't get back until about noon Monday. We then spent the night together and Sunny introduced me to oral sex, yet one more thing that I'm probably years behind my peers in experiencing. Honestly, I didn't even realize that people did things like that to each other.

I now will have a whole new frame of reference when I hear someone ask, "Do you kiss your mother with that mouth?"

Back in college, though, is when I first discovered that certain parts of the human anatomy have optional uses. In a novel by Gore Vidal, **Myra Breckenridge**, I learned how gay guys have sex. At first, I kept trying to visualize how one guy could stick his penis inside another's. Then, suddenly, the clouds parted, the sun beamed down, and I saw the light.

Holy cow!

Sunny attended UCLA, where she studied journalism. So we have the latter in common. She's also one of the most talented and enthusiastic people I've ever met—right up there with Grace for the enthusiasm.

Her father was actor Frank Sully. He died of cancer a year ago Christmas, and Sunny has had a difficult time adjusting to the loss.

In addition to being an actor in hundreds of TV programs and movies, he evidently also was a larger than life character and, perhaps, a bit of a lovable con man. He ran an acting school for children. He used to buy costume jewelry at department stores and then have "estate" sales.

So… I can't help but wonder how much daughter is like father. I guess I'll find out.

Sunny is extremely perceptive. She already knows me better than most, and I feel the same about her. We tease one another frequently, knowing just how the other will respond.

Of course, with a name like Kathleen Honora Sullivan, she's Irish, and proud of it.

Oh, yes, only about a week ago, Grace and I had a talk because I was feeling a little depressed. She said someone would come along, someone special. She said it probably would happen through my job. Then my editor transferred a call from Sunny Sullivan to me, asking me to do a story about her and her new business venture.

As Grace would say, "Isn't that incredible?"

May 5, Tallahassee

Pepper the cocker spaniel earned $15,000 last year. The dog could buy its own Cadillac. She also supposedly was the first dog used in Coppertone ads and commercials. I must admit, though, this revelation set off my BS detector and I'm starting to wonder how much I'm being told from the Hollywood crowd is true.

Earl, a good friend and photographer at the paper, told me tonight about a paraplegic midget. Evidently, a story ran on the guy last fall. He was living in a tent out off Highway 20, and using crutches to get around. He had a pet dog until the story ran and people started driving out to see if they could help him. One of them ran over the dog.

By the way, I seem to relate to and get along with photographers much better than reporters. I'm not sure what that says about them or me. But from what I've observed, photographers are more unconventional and independent than reporters, and don't care about their appearances nearly so much. They also see things that average people don't.

May 9, Tallahassee

I spent the weekend in Pensacola with Sunny, where she has another store. That's when we decided to run away to the Bahamas together.

Grace asked me today if I am in love. I said, "Ah, yeah."

I also told her I was uncertain of its permanence, which is stupid. After all, when beginning a relationship, nobody knows about its permanence. I guess that statement shows how much I want it to be permanent.

Grace's thoughts on the subject: Love doesn't stay the same. It changes and grows. Just let it become.

I also told her that Sunny and I are being very impractical. She said it's too boring to be practical. "You wind up old and gray and watching television eight hours a day," she said.

May 20, Tallahassee

It was a tough day for Sunny. She was supposed to turn her VW van over to the bank since she used it as collateral on a loan to get the store started. Since she hasn't been able to make payments, the bank closed the store more than a week ago. She also hasn't been paying rent to her landlord, Ruby Pearl Diamond. Yeah, that's why we're planning on heading to the Bahamas, ahead of her pursuing creditors. Florida's capital city just isn't ready for a gallery/art store, I guess.

Early in the day, Sunny said she was bad for me. She said books had been written about such ill-fated romances. I said, "Yes, but the author determines the romance is ill-fated."

She replied, "Who's the author?"

Good question.

When I stopped by her house later in the day, I told her I suspected she had thoughts of skipping town and just leaving a letter for me. I told her I would quit my job and go after her. She then told me she had written a letter and left it in some of my laundry on the table. But she took the letter back.

"You know me too well," she said. "I'm not sure I like that."

Still later, she said the bank had agreed to let her keep the van until tomorrow at noon. She's talking as if she won't turn it in tomorrow.

We spent the evening with Grace, the twins, and their friends, Chris and Dick, who helped bolster our spirits. We talked a little about the Caribbean, as well as bouncing back from defeat. Dick looks at defeat as an impetus to go in a new direction.

Chris said she was down to her last $10 once. So, she dropped the money in the toilet and flushed it away. That eliminated the problem of trying to decide what to do with it.

They told stories about Sunny's landlord, Ruby Pearl Diamond, who is 90 years old and living in a downtown hotel. I can't vouch for the truthfulness of any of them, but they are doozies:

Ruby once evicted karate students from her building and kept their sign. She later tried to sell it back to them.

She sold antiques and then called buyers up later and said she didn't charge enough.

She decided to hold a going-out-of-business sale in her china shop. She charged 50 cents admission. When people got inside, they discovered the china was still priced too high. But Ruby profited from the admissions.

Finally, she has one eye and a $3.95 nose. She was too cheap to have doctors build her a nose after a bout with cancer.

*****

After we headed back to my basement apartment, Sunny said that she couldn't leave the store as it was, with the works there of so many artists who had trusted her. "I don't know if they'll ever get them back," she said.

And since she had her van for only one more night…

In the wee, small hours of pre-dawn, I began my life of crime with Kathleen Honora Sullivan. Clad all in black, we broke into the back of the store. Staying in the shadows as much as possible, we crept around on tiptoes, carefully carrying the consignment works out of the store and loading them into the van. Occasionally, we couldn't avoid exposure from the glow of a street light out front, and, more than a few times, I was certain that passing motorists, including a couple of police cars, must have seen us. But no sirens sounded. No arrests were made.

And, I'm ashamed to admit, the adrenaline rush I received during those electric 90 minutes or so was as pleasurable as any I experienced while playing sports.

Oh, Hell, maybe I wasn't supposed to be a writer after. Maybe my calling is cat burglar. I've just had a good start on my apprenticeship.

May 26, Tallahassee

Up yours, 9 to 5! Or, in my case, 8 to 4.

I gave two weeks' notice today at the newspaper. It didn't go well after that. Editors who hired me just three months ago were not pleased, and I certainly understand that. What made it even tougher for me is that I respect them and am appreciative of them giving me a second chance at the paper.

Of course, I never should have gone back. That's backtracking and not what I'm about right now. I want to go forward to experiences and opportunities. But following a month of sleeping on a rented bed in my friends' living room, I needed to make money, to start paying my own way.

So what's different now? Well, for one thing, I can make money by helping John Lee write that time management book, and he's given me his lake home rent-free for the summer.

For another, there's Sunny. I suspect that she's not going to stay around here much longer, especially since our crime caper. Considering that she has that second store in Pensacola, I believe that she owes money to a few people other than her landlord here in Tallahassee, and they're going to start complicating her life if she stays around here.

And since we've already talked about running away to the Bahamas… At this point, I'm not sure what that means, but it sounds good to me—at least until the "heat blows over," so to speak. I still want to work with John on his book, while living at the lake and working on my own, so I don't want to be in exile permanently.

But on the other hand, who knows what awaits in the Bahamas?

Of course, I didn't mention Sunny to the editors, but I did give my desire to write books as a reason for my departure.

One of them said that he's known a lot of people who wanted to write books, but few who actually did.

The other said that ending my weekly column, "Must Be Monday," will make both me and them look stupid.

I don't think that "stupid" is the right word, but I can't argue that my departure is not a good look for both the paper and me.

Still, I truly believe that saying goodbye to the newspaper business—permanently this time—is what's best for me.

I went home after I talked to the editors and Sunny put me on the phone with her mother out in L.A., who also is a writer. She said some wonderful things that enabled me to open up and cry a few minutes later.

She said people told her similar things when she decided to be the manager of her own time. They said if she wasn't working in an office and contributing, she wasn't doing anything worthwhile. She said she works 18 hours in a row sometimes, and she feels good about it because her time is her own.

She also said I couldn't deny myself. I had to do what I was born to do. And, if I didn't, it would be tragic.

*****

Sunny asked me last night if we might have a child "when we grow up." I said, "Yes." I never felt that way before, and now I realize it's because I never had met anyone I wanted to have a child with—even my ex-wife.

Sunny said that when she was 5 or 6, she used to run down the block at 6 a.m., clad in her father's tee shirt down to her ankles, yelling "Something's happening! Something's happening! And it's wonderful!"

The neighbors didn't approve.

She's been a run-away all her life, she said, starting at age 4. She made it all the way into Burbank once by telling a driver she was from Burbank and had been kidnapped.

Society, she said, "is always trying to kill my child."

She also admitted that she's almost run away from Tallahassee several times because of problems with the store, something I suspected all along.

On Sunday, Sunny even went so far as to call my friend Linda at the paper and ask her to drive her to the airport. Linda took her home for dinner and Sunny later called me to come and get her.

She said she's staying because of me. And I know that's causing her considerable conflict because she never has felt so tied to anyone before.

*****

My brother, Craig, and his friend, Jim, arrived Monday, and the Mayfields and I really are enjoying having them visit. I see so much of how I was at 20 in Craig. It's both reassuring and disconcerting. But I think I'm turning out all right—said the man who just committed a crime—so he probably will too.

June 2, On the Road

Oh, yeah! After I sold my MGB, Sunny and I blew town in a 1959 VW bus that she bought for $300. We headed toward Tampa to pick up her mother and her second husband at the airport. From there… who knows? Well, I don't anyway.

During a Florida shower, we discovered that the roof leaks. And then came the really fun part. At an intersection just north of Homosassa Springs, I put my foot on the brake pedal to stop at a traffic light—and we coasted on through. Fortunately, traffic was light and no one slammed into us from the side.

No brakes! Well, we had almost no brakes. By slowing down and constantly keeping my foot pressed on the pedal I discovered I could semi-control the bus, maybe until we could at least get to a gas station.

But it wasn't to be. Finally the brakes went out completely and I stopped us by veering off the road and bumping into a metal pole and then a tree. Fortunately, I was going so slow that we weren't hurt. And, not that it mattered, the bus didn't seem to be either.

From there, we hiked on down the road a bit to the Old Mill Tavern. A woman at the door introduced us to Jimmy Huggins, a 29-year-old good, ol' boy sign painter whose wife up and went to Oklahoma. Jimmy poured his whiskey in a plastic cup and went out to take at look at the VW.

After spilling his drink on the seat and crawling around underneath the bus, he diagnosed the problem as a busted wheel cylinder. He told us that the only place that worked on VWs was Chuck's. And he told us how to get there: Down the street to the post office, then left at Juanita's Beauty Salon.

But before we left, we went back into the tavern to buy Jimmy another drink, since he spilled the one he had.

He told us about eating gator tails, hunting gators from a pink Lincoln Continental in an orange orchard, and sharks. Jimmy doesn't eat shark meat. One of his friends was eaten by a shark, he said, and "there was only 30 pounds of him left. They stuffed him in a 30-gallon garbage bag."

After reading **Jaws**, Jimmy stopped swimming in the ocean. "Your skin gets soft and even those big ol' needlefish start biting you," he said.

Jimmy said he helped rescue a girl who floated 15 miles offshore. He's the one who spotted her. "The Coast Guard kept asking what she was wearing and my brother was saying, 'She's nekid! She's nekid!'"

Jimmy told us the story was in **Reader's Digest**. "But I wrote a letter and told 'em if they want to know the real story, I'll be glad to tell 'em," he said.

Finally, after a couple more shots all around, Jimmy hopped in his '69 Roadrunner and guided us—very slowly—to Chuck's. He then dropped us off at the Springs Motel.

At this point, I'm not sure how we're going to get to Tampa in two days to pick up Sunny's mother. Well, I wanted adventure…

June 8, Venice, Fla.

Well, what do you know? The bus got fixed and we picked up Sunny's mother and stepfather on time. Since then, we've been staying in a rented bungalow near the beach, which her mother arranged in advance.

Walking along the water's edge for a couple of hours each day, I've collected a couple of pounds of fossilized shark teeth. And in talking to people, I've discovered that this is sort of the unofficial world epicenter for such findings.

Sunny's mother also is going to buy a house here. Huh. I'm not sure why, and it's none of my business. But house-hunting has helped pass the time as well.

My guess is that that we'll visit for awhile longer and then Sunny and I will head south, ever closer to the Bahamas. Right now, I'm being pretty compliant and just enjoying the ride.

Here's a story I overheard while having lunch at Fisherman's Wharf: Some guys tied a shark line to the front bumper of their pickup. A shark took the bait and then started pulling the truck into the water, although the wheels were locked. One of the guys hopped in the pickup, put it in reverse, and slammed down the gas pedal. It did no good, as the shark kept dragging the truck farther and farther into the water. Finally, they cut the line.

And here's some interesting gossip from a travel agent friend of Sunny's mother: A 14-year-old boy was sexually assaulted in an elevator during a trip to Hawaii. And that's where authorities found the tip of the man's tongue. The boy also broke his arm when he brought it down on the man's head. The police said it wouldn't be hard to find the man, since he likely would be bleeding heavily.

Probably he wouldn't be saying much either.

During the same trip, a drunken woman got mad at her husband and decided to swim to the group's next stop—Tahiti. She was four miles out when the Coast Guard pulled her aboard.

*****

I talked to Grace last night. Broward Taft, the head of the bank, is looking for both Sunny and me. Yikes! When he went to the paper, someone told him that Grace is a friend, so he contacted her. She said that he started looking for us the same day we left. So, now I'm a criminal and a fugitive from justice whose only material wealth at the moment are a couple of bags of fossilized shark teeth.

Nevertheless, staying at the beach really has put me in a pleasant frame of mind. I think I'd like living by the ocean.

Even though we're on the lam together, Sunny and I still haven't definitely determined that we have a long-term future with each other. I guess that I hope we do. But I also know that I have a lot to resolve inside me before I'm the person I want to be—and maybe the person she could live with.

Sunny is a free spirit, an anachronism, someone who refuses to be structured by society. Is that what I want? As I write this, I'm not sure. It's so difficult to separate my feelings for Sunny from how I truly feel about all of this craziness going on right now. Add to that, I'm not so sure that Sunny can live with anyone.

We'll see, I guess.

June 11, Tallahassee

Sunny and I went our separate ways today at the Sarasota airport. I flew back to Tallahassee to live at Lake Ellen for the summer and help John Lee with his time management book. And Sunny is going to the Bahamas alone.

Well, I guess she is going to the Bahamas. That's what she says, anyway. With her, who knows?

She said that she loves me "but it won't work."

After what she did that last night, she doesn't have to tell me that. I could see it for myself.

During the week that we spent with her mother in Venice, Sunny gave me many reasons our relationship wouldn't work long-term. Some of them were valid, I think, but most seemed more designed to convince herself rather than me that we should split up. She was determined to run away, and not just from Tallahassee and debt, but from me as well. By verbalizing, she could more easily rationalize.

She said that I'm angry, critical, and uncommunicative. She said I'm the first person she's ever put as her first priority, but I haven't done the same.

On the way to the airport, Sunny said that she thinks she is "just a topic" for me, and that I'm in the relationship because it's advantageous. She said that she knows everything that goes on in my mind, but I have as much insight into her as a plastic fork.

Well, I have enough insight to at least suspect that she's afraid of an intimate relationship. Words weren't enough to push me away, though. So, last night, she delivered the coup de grace with her actions.

During dinner at a restaurant, Sunny seemed extremely agitated. Finally, she left the table. The three of us thought she was going to the restroom. But she never returned.

After waiting an extra half-hour for her to come back, we drove the 12 miles back to our rental. A motorcycle was parked out front and two helmets were on the ground. No one was in the villa, but the smell of grass was almost overpowering.

Sunny came in about 10 minutes later, and I heard the motorcycle leave about the same time. She then went directly to bed without saying anything.

She didn't want to talk this morning either. Her mother's husband and I suspected that maybe she and her mother had quarreled. We were wrong.

Finally, I confronted Sunny and asked what was going on. Her first response was, "It won't work." Then she said, "Our timing is lousy," adding that if we'd met two years before or two years later, she'd be willing to work at the relationship. But now, she said, she didn't have the patience.

"No problem," I replied. "You convinced me last night with that stunt you pulled. Being a free spirit is one thing. Running away without telling me what was going on is another.

"You're right. Our relationship won't work," I said. "But it's not because of timing. It's because you were determined to push me away and you succeeded. Congratulations.

"You took off last night with no regard for the worry and concern you would cause for those who care about you. And I'm not interested in having a serious relationship with someone capable of pulling stunts like that."

I'm not sure how I feel about her now. There's an empty, hollow feeling inside. I don't feel compelled to forget her, or to write her an angry letter, or maybe even a passionate one. So much is going on inside her head right now. She needs time to rest and set priorities.

Or maybe not. That could be just wishful thinking on my part. Maybe that's just who she is, now and forever. If so, I'm grateful to her for showing me now, instead of waiting until we got to the Bahamas.

Although I still have a lot of growing up to do, what I do know is that I'd never do anything so disrespectful to another person, especially someone I professed to care about.

The bottom line, I suspect, is she didn't want it to work and, while I'm hurt, as well as exhausted from the chaos that's been swirling around us for awhile now,

I'm okay with that. So while she sorts out her life in the Bahamas, I'll do the same on Lake Ellen.

*****

I told Mom that I quit my job, and there was this deafening silence on the other end of the line. She has no conception at all of my wanting to write books. Last week, when I told her I was considering quitting newspaper work to write a book, she said, "Then what would you do?"

Thank God I have the Mayfields to talk with. I'm not certain I could confront my feelings if they weren't around to help. I need them to help keep me from withdrawing into a shell and not talking.

Filming starts soon in Tallahassee for **Hank**, the movie Rachel is starring in. Well, supposedly it will. After my recent experience with Sunny, who grew up in that Hollywood atmosphere and now is in exile in the Bahamas, I'm starring to have my doubts about the credibility of Michael Musto. I have no evidence, though, so I'll just keep my mouth shut.

Grace told me that Rachel and Rebecca were invited to a luncheon because the mother of the hostess found out Rachel was going to be in a movie. The twins declined. Rachel said the girl who invited them brings an alphabetized list of her Christmas presents to school each year.

Rachel and Rebecca also told me about babysitting at Blessed Sacrament School. The little children, they said, often fall into the toilet and they have to pull them out.

I'd say that's an apt metaphor for life in general and why we need friends and family around us.

June 20, Lake Ellen

I moved to the lake yesterday. John had hinted that he might do so as well, to facilitate our work. But he hasn't, and he said that he's having problems with his truck and his boat, which I guess means he wants to get those fixed before coming down.

He got the truck stuck in the sand yesterday, while trying to get the boat out to have it fixed.

A distant neighbor, Bill, helped dig the truck out and I asked him about the fishing. He took it from there.

He was "catfishin'" with his brother from Wisconsin last November, he said, when Bill spied a 5-foot alligator. He told his brother that he was going to put it in the boat. His brother replied, "No, you're not."

"I pulled the gator in over the side and he went over the other," Bill said.

I've seen several gators already, most of them in the evenings.

Dusk is beautiful on and around the lake. As the sun slides away, the cypress trees turn to silhouettes and the blue sky burns away to black. Ospreys and herons fly home in the twilight, and soon the glee club starts. Frogs cheep, chirp, and croak all around the lake, with absolutely no ear for harmony, yet the chorus is beautiful nonetheless. Feeding fish dimple the lake's glassy surface.

The fishing has been good—three catfish and two bass—and I've seen rabbits, squirrels, and a snake. A cow seems to visit daily. The grass is greener here, evidently. While I watched this afternoon, she headed down toward the lake, a cattle egret perched on her back.

June 21, Tallahassee

Grace suggested today that my brother might now consider coming down here to live, since Sunny won't be coming back to Tallahassee. I said that I couldn't handle that right now because I'm tired of working. She knew what I meant, working at relationships, and she said that I should remember that for my novel.

She is my biggest booster, constantly talking to me about reading and writing. Today she suggested I might build a small place to live and work in at the back of their property.

Also, she talked some more about Jim, her mentally ill ex-husband. When he was 8, he wrote to chemical companies across the country, said he was conducting a study, and asked for sample of their products. A UPS truck pulled up to his home one day "with enough barrels to blow up Pittsburgh." With some of the products, she said, he built rockets.

Jim was fascinated with aerosols and that partially helped the minister at their church see Jim was not normal. He was "spraying roaches" in the bathroom one day while the minister was there and told him how he liked to spray, close the cabinets, and then listen to the roaches scurrying.

*****

Now that I'm at the lake south of Tallahassee, I'm going to try to work on my own novel and a few magazine pieces, as well as John's book, which he has entitled **Manuel DeMayfly**. Adult mayflies live very short lives, some species for only a day, and I'm guessing John wants to use that to emphasize the importance of wise time management. But I don't know for sure. He hasn't provided me with details. He hasn't had the time. For someone who's made such a success of telling others how to manage their time, how well he manages his own certainly is questionable.

He doesn't even take the time to do laundry. He just buys new underwear.

John also has given me the use of a car that he keeps at the lake so I can come and go as I please. I'm the only one living at the lake house. He stays in Tallahassee with his girlfriend, Cathy.

Sunny sent me a card from the Bahamas. "There are so many answers. If only I could match them up with the questions, the feelings, and the individual convictions," she said. "Then, if we could combine them! Oh, what a match we'd make. I don't know if that will ever occur. But I love you."

That's an easy thing to tell someone when you're hundreds of miles apart, with no prospect of ever seeing one another again.

I don't love her. I've searched and searched for a reason to. I'd like to love her, but she's too ephemeral. She's really, as she says, "not a real person." She reveals only bits and pieces, and, often, they come reluctantly.

She's certainly a good character to write about though.

Some of the accusations she leveled at me—not loving her, although she loves me. Not knowing how to love anyone—I just read about in a book, **The Magus**, by John Fowles, which Sunny left behind. I told Grace that I thought maybe I was just being paranoid. She said using content from a book was typical of Sunny's type character, whatever type she is.

Grace said Sunny's life seems to be "non-purposive." I agreed, but I also think much of Sunny's energy is used up running away.

I now believe Sunny has just as much to learn about herself as I do about me. The Hell with that! I think she has more.

That's not why I don't love her, but it's related. The issues she has within herself make it impossible for her to lay her soul bare to someone and say, "This is me." She rebels every step of the way if an intimate relationship seems to be developing. She refuses to allow herself to be loved, and, right now, I just don't feel like fighting. I want to get on with my life.

Oh, if it were only as easy to psycho-analyze myself as I just did Sunny.

I still don't feel ready to write about The Incident involving Sunny and Craig. But now that I've said that, I suddenly feel freer to do so.

On Monday, May 30, Sunny woke Craig and Jim up by throwing water on them in my apartment. Jim took it as a joke, laughed, and threw some water on Sunny. Craig never smiled, and he even chased Sunny in his Bronco when she left in her VW.

Later at the Mayfields, Sunny turned the sprinkler on Craig and Jim. After she did it a second time, Craig got her in a headlock, stuck her head in the spray, and held it there, saying, "Have you had enough?" He seemed almost maniacal.

It was ugly. Sunny went in the house crying and I went in to comfort her. I then went for a walk with Craig. As soon as we got away from the house, he started crying. Try as I might, I couldn't convince him we weren't mad at him. I tried talking to him about feelings and told him not to let things build up inside.

I had my arm around his shoulders and it felt good to talk with him about feelings, a subject that never was discussed at home. Also, the default emotion for any situation was anger. In fact, that's the only emotion I can recall from my father, except when he is drunk.

About three hours later, after banana splits at the Mayfields, Sunny approached Craig and said she wanted to talk about her feelings. Her timing probably was bad, since both Jim and I where there, and we were in the Mayfields' driveway. Instantly, Craig went on the defensive. He started crying and said he and Jim were going to my place to pack and leave that night.

I followed him. We yelled at one another. He said what he did was him and he couldn't do anything about it. I asked him if he wanted to grow up and be just like Dad. He said, "If that's me… "

He then said, "If you want to know, I never did like her." He complained because she asked them to help her move some things the day they arrived, and they agreed. I told him to be mad at himself, not her.

That part of him is just like Mom: do whatever anyone wants you to do, whether you want to or not, and then bitch about it to someone else. I tried and tried to tell him to use his head, to make his own decisions, and to express his feelings.

We hugged, he cried, and I did a little, too. And they left. I pray something good will come out of this.

The last time I remember anything so frightening was when Dad lost his temper and beat me on my back and bottom with a belt and belt buckle when I was maybe 9. It was a display of anger totally disproportionate to what I had done—accidently spilled a glass of milk at the breakfast table. And, I belatedly discovered, that rage has instilled in me a fear of him ever since, even though I'm now an adult. When we're in the same room together, I always sit as far away from him as possible.

When you're a child, I guess, you accept anything that happens to you as "normal." I didn't realize that beating was abusive behavior until I wrote that article about child abuse, even though I had red welts all over my back as a result.

That same type temper is in Craig, and he must learn to deal with it before someone is seriously hurt.

Also, he never had been confronted by a woman before, as Sunny did him in the Mayfields' driveway. Always before, I suspect, he had experienced only women like mother and my sister, women who do what they're supposed to and keep their mouths shut. Now Craig knows that whole world is not like that. I hope he can learn and grow from that revelation.

June 24, Tallahassee

Grace showed me the family's Christmas present to Karen this year. It's a book, hand-written by Grace. At the Mayfields, each person receives one gift. Solicited presents aren't allowed.

That's quite a change from my family, where solicited gifts were mandatory. Each year, Mom insisted on knowing what we wanted, and then she went overboard, buying and wrapping dozens and dozens of gifts. I'm beginning to suspect that's a way of compensating when you don't know how to express your love through words and actions.

Karen's book includes a passage recalling Grace's thoughts when Karen was born and a portion entitled "On Being Karen's Mother." There's one called "About 42." That number is the code grace and Karen use to tell one another "I love you." It's especially useful after quarrels. They convey the message without saying the words.

The book also includes lists of places they have lived and pets they've had, as well as Karen's favorite foods and favorite things to do—meatloaf and string beans and listen to music and rock in a chair.

Grace said she's going to add recipes of Karen's favorite foods and whatever else she feels moved to include.

I think it's the best, most loving present I've ever heard of.

The Mayfields gave me a Siamese fighting fish last night, "as a love gift." I was very appreciative, but couldn't help laughing at the paradox. A "kissing gourami" might have been more appropriate, considering my encounter with the "kissing disease" earlier this year.

*****

I received a letter today from Sunny in the Bahamas. She still says she loves me. I've still got an empty feeling inside.

June 26, Tallahassee

Grace, Doug, and I saw the movie **Sorcerer** last night. It's based on Georgs Arnaud's 1953 novel, ***Wages of Fear,*** and definitely is one of the most powerful films I've seen. It was difficult to move when it was over, to think, to see, to react.

The movie put violence and fear in perspective, instead of candy-coating it as is done in most films and on television. Four people entered a violent world through criminal acts and found violence begets violence, with fear as a constant shadow.

Our discussion of the film led to talk of living life intensely, since death is always just behind, shining its headlights into your rearview mirror as it keeps pace to prevent your escape.

Grace talked of the film ***Zorba the Greek*** and how Zorba lived life to the fullest, enjoying wine, women, dancing, and living spontaneously.

I wonder how Zorba differs from Sunny. Supposedly, she lives spontaneously, doing what she wants when she wants. And I've said I want to be the way she is. Something bothered me about my saying that, and now I think I've put my finger on it.

Zorba's spontaneity, from what Grace said, was enthusiastic. Sunny's seems to be out of resignation, as if she has no other recourse than to be spontaneous, which seems sort of a contradiction.

I don't want that sort of spontaneity. I don't want to be bound by it. I want it to be a part of me, not the sum of my being.

And, too, Zorba was simplistic. He revealed what he liked and what he wanted out of life. I don't think Sunny knows either one of those things, or, if she does, she won't reveal them.

After I received her letter, she called me. Remembering that Grace had used the term to describe Sunny, I told her I thought her life was "non-purposive." That incited the most fervent response of anything I said, which, I guess, was my objective.

"How can you say that?" she screamed.

I also told her she seemed determined to run away from any lasting relationships, and she admitted her mother had told her the same. Although I didn't tell her, I suspect that she has made it her personal belief that love means suffering a self-fulfilling prophecy.

I told her I thought many of her accusations were bullshit that she was using to build a wall between us so she might easier escape.

Putting aside her one outburst, she seemed to take everything I said pretty well, and I felt better about her and myself when I had finished.

At the end of the conversation, I said, "I have this big urge to say, 'I love you.' But I'm not going to."

I know there can be no deep and intimate relationship for us. She's terrifically uplifting to be around, for awhile anyway, but terribly sad to ponder.

July 2, Lake Ellen

I just spent a very enjoyable, but unplanned, two days with the Mayfields. Their car broke down on the way back from picking up Linda at Camp Weed, which is down this way. After Doug and I spent all afternoon getting the car to the lake house, I drove them back into Tallahassee.

Linda, who just turned 16, broke up with her boyfriend last night, and the two of us spent the next morning talking about that. I hope it helped for her to talk to me. It must have. She kissed me goodbye tonight.

Grace and I spent the afternoon driving all over the city in the car John loaned me, delivering and picking up girls here and there.

With the car finally fixed late tonight, Doug and Grace now are on their way home.

*****

I'm hoping that John and I begin work on his time management book tomorrow. I'm really eager to get started. And I'm starting work on my novel too.

The freedom I now have to run my own life is almost frightening, but frightening only because it is a new experience. All I have to do is set up a writing schedule, according to my own needs and wants, not someone else's time clock. Most people, I think, don't want the responsibility of actually controlling their own lives. They'd rather have a lifestyle organized by society. Then they have something or someone to blame when they're unhappy or unsuccessful or not rich enough.

Sometime soon, I think I'd like someone to share life with. But right now, I'm enjoying being by myself to think and write and fish or just watch an alligator glide by under an idyllic sunset. This summer, I'm sure, is going to be something special.

July 6, Lake Ellen

There's something in the chimney of the fireplace in my bedroom. Maybe it's a family of owls. For the past two nights, I've heard fluttering sounds and choruses of "cheeps."

I haven't talked to anyone today, and I just found out why. The phone isn't working.

John was supposed to come back out, but he didn't. I'm going to have to press him a little harder. He's given me some information, but not nearly enough to start writing the book. He's supposed to be my primary source. I'll have to remind him of that.

I stayed in town on the 4th and took Linda to the movies. She's still having boyfriend problems. Chris is crazy if he leaves her. She still loves him, she said. But he's feeling all sorts of conflicts about what he wants and how to express his feelings. I can sympathize. But as a biased observer, I don't think that Linda deserves the run-around he is giving her.

Doug told me that when Grace was a little girl, her brother and a friend of his convinced her to set her doll in the fire. They told her it wouldn't hurt the doll. How cruel is that?

When she was a teen he also revealed, Grace has rheumatic fever and was forced to stay in bed for a year.

*****

July 12, Lake Ellen

My friends Dave and Shirley visited last week. Linda and Rebecca will be here tomorrow for a few days. My parents will arrive this weekend. Despite the interruptions, I need to put in time on John's book. The novel also needs work.

I've had thoughts today about wanting to "live" rather than write. By that I mean travel and experience whatever comes my way. To be honest, though, I think that those thoughts are little more than procrastination, the infamous roadblock to accomplishment that so many would-be writers succumb to. Before I moved here, I kept telling myself I would start writing as soon as I arrived. I have—to a degree. But I need to do more.

I'm not sure anymore why I want to write. But then I've never really known. Now, however, I feel a deep desire to put my world into words, which is not quite the same. Before, I think, being a writer was something I wanted, but without feeling it inside. It's funny how talking about your "novel" starts the process rolling and, pretty soon, you're involved. At least that's the way it works for me. Now, there is a need to eat, sleep, make love—and write.

The Mayfields have told me I can stay in their home for as long as I need, while getting started as a self-employed writer. Grace, bless her, is my biggest fan.

John is talking about my working with him for more than this first book. But thus far, I've been less than impressed with his commitment to that. As a time management expert, he's not doing so well with his own time. I'll just have to wait and see.

I feel a great jubilance about life now and feel now is the time to make things happen.

July 18, Lake Ellen

My parents visited Friday through Sunday. Having the Mayfields around really helped my attitude. But I still started getting depressed Sunday afternoon.

Slowly, but surely, I'm learning to accept my parents, but it's not easy. I want them to be so much more than they are. But that never will happen, which is what I have to come to terms with. And I also have to accept the fact I'll never be able to talk about feelings with them.

Doug said my father is the perfect example of chronic depression. And Grace mentioned both how often my Mom says my father loves us "kids" and how she maneuvers all around an issue instead of saying what she wants. Grace said Doug's mother acts the same way. The former, she believes, is said to alleviate guilt feelings. The latter to avoid confrontation or rejection.

As an example, when my mother wanted sugar to cook with and found too little in the Mayfields' kitchen, she asked, "Which neighbors do you borrow from?"

Grace likes my mother, and thinks she is a heroic person, along with most other mothers of that generation.

Linda said I wasn't at all like my family, and Rachel said "your father sure is different."

*****

Rachel met with Mr. Musto on Sunday, and he talked about her starring in a television series. But now filming of the movie won't start until August. Hmmm. More and more, I have my doubts about whether it ever will happen. Of course, my judgment now is colored by getting involved with the ethereal daughter of a Hollywood actor who sold costume jewelry at "estate sales."

On my way into town Thursday, I looked down at my feet and saw a baby bird hopping between the brake and gas pedals. Yikes!

Somehow I managed to pull to the side of the road without stepping on it. It was a robin. Then I took it on to Tallahassee with me for the day, before returning it to the lake and releasing it on Friday.

I'm guessing the little guy had a great story to tell his brothers and sisters.

How could I forget? On Friday, Grace told me that a lump has been found in her right breast. She hadn't even told Doug, she said, because too many things are going on right now to burden him with something else. She said the doctor believes the lump isn't anything serious. Test results were supposed to be back today. I forgot to ask her about the results when she called today.

July 25, Lake Ellen

Grace is okay. At least she said she's okay.

I spent the weekend in town, and came back out late this afternoon, after a dentist appointment and a movie with Linda, Rachel, and Rebecca.

John and I finally are here at the same time. So what happens? Fiasco.

I helped launch his boat at the public landing, only for him to discover that he didn't have the key. He had to go back to the house for that. Then, as he drove the boat over to his dock, I got the truck and trailer stuck in the sand. We now are tied for that dubious accomplishment, twice each.

I've been thinking about going to Flat River to work on my novel, after John and I finish the mayfly book. It seems to be so appealing, and that's what I can't understand. I'd quickly become depressed up there and go into a blue funk. Why do I constantly want to go back, only to be disappointed? The attraction, I guess, is having lived there for four years, the longest time I've lived anywhere during my 28 years.

And my family is there, even though I do seem to be so different from them. I'm sure security feelings are tied up in there somewhere, fed by blood relationships and sense of place.

I will visit Flat River, though. I enjoy it for a little while at least. And it's a great source of story material.

It took awhile to get started out here, but I think I've finally gotten myself motivated.

I'm still hearing cheeps in the chimney, only now they're more frequent than before. I hope that I'm not about to be treated to a real life episode of Alfred Hitchcock's ***The Birds***.

July 26, Lake Ellen

Another misadventure with John today. He wanted to try out the boat he had just had fixed for the second straight time, as well as a slalom ski that he received as a birthday present.

With the boat parallel to shore, and Cathy and me in it, John was standing in about three feet of water with his back to the shore, trying to untangle the ski rope.

"John, look behind you at…," I said.

Not even bothering to look, he catapulted himself into the boat with a horrified look on his face. Of course, he thought I was warning him about an approaching gator. I wasn't.

He acted so quickly that he didn't hear what else I said: "…that pig."

As soon as he splashed aboard, he turned around and saw what Cathy and I had seen, a large porker strolling nonchalantly down the beach.

The boat didn't work—again. The motor wouldn't generate enough power to pull John up onto the ski. Once, it almost did. But the rope broke.

As we circled around to pick him up, I saw a small gator about 20 feet from him. Since it posed no threat at all, I should have kept my mouth shut. I did not.

Once again he launched himself into the boat. Poor John.

Today, I retyped a short story and an essay about my adventure with mono, in preparation to mail them when I go into town the next time. So far, no luck freelancing, but I'll keep sending stuff "over the transom."

July 27, Lake Ellen

With the moon almost full, I decided to go fishing tonight. I didn't catch any fish, but certainly enjoyed some excitement. A gator exploded on my surface lure and streaked away. Almost all of my line was gone before the bait finally pulled out of his mouth.

Until tonight, I had no idea so many gators were in this lake. They were everywhere, swimming, splashing, and slapping their tails on the surface as they dived. Back in the shadows, dozens of gator eyes glowed like bicycle reflectors. Maybe John had been wise not to linger in the water.

Aug. 4, Lake Ellen

Not much to report. John was sick for a couple of days. Then, so was I. John and Cathy have gone to Disney World, where he is giving a day-long presentation tomorrow.

I've sent out several queries for time management-related articles. I've also written a little on the mayfly book. I plan to spend much of tomorrow working on it.

Nature put on a light show tonight. The stars were extremely bright, reflecting off the lake as if it were a mirror. Lightning illuminated the horizon on three sides, and falling stars flashed by now and then.

Grace called tonight. She wants me to meet a woman who's faced with divorce and having a tough time coping. Her husband, Grace said, just won't talk. Grace wondered aloud why people insist on inflicting suffering on others.

Grace has a pain in her side, and is going to see the doctor about it Monday. One ovary was left in when she had her hysterectomy, and the doctor told her at the time that eventually it would have to come out.

Aug. 14, Lake Ellen

What the Hell is so difficult about being a writer? I might have no talent and nothing to say, but that hasn't stopped others. I've got everything going for me, it seems, except publication.

My mother called today to say that I wouldn't have to have a job if I wanted to come up there to write. "We could feed you," she said. "Dad says we throw out more than you would eat."

The Mayfields want me to live with them and write. Grace called tonight to encourage me to submit 50 pages of my novel to Houghton Mifflin, a publishing company that offers $10,000 awards.

But I have the lake house here at least through September, and the atmosphere is great for writing.

I just received three rejection slips from magazines. But **The Floridian** asked to see more of my work.

Of course she's prejudiced, but Grace said I'm good enough to get a book published, and she thinks I have something to say. I sure hope so.

And I sure hope I can stop thinking and talking and dreaming about writing and actually do it!!!

Aug. 17, Lake Ellen

I haven't felt compelled to write in the journal lately, and there's not much to report. I'm hoping to get 50 pages of my novel done by the end of September so that I can submit it to Houghton Mifflin. And I'm trying to get the mayfly book done by then too. The big stumbling block there is John. He's still disorganized in his own life, as he tells others how to organize theirs. But he's improving. Or is that just wishful thinking on my part?

I experienced a new sensation tonight, a sweet, fruity fragrance wafted out onto the dock. It was almost intoxicating. I finally figured out the aroma was coming from the grape arbor. It made me feel as if I were in France or Italy at harvest time.

I'm spending lots of time on the dock, especially in the evenings. Sometimes I fish. Other times I just rock.

After the nude sunbathing episode there a couple of weeks ago, I decided to avoid it during the day. I never knew what pain was until I experienced a sunburned penis.

Aug. 31, Lake Ellen

As I keep trying to corral John to work on the mayfly book, he's now talking enthusiastically about our doing a five-part film series on time management.

I just wrote a short story based on an old hotel south of Blountstown. It's for sale, and John wanted to take a look at it. The wife wants to sell, but the husband doesn't. It reminded me of the hotel in the Bogart movie **Key Largo**, only without the approaching hurricane.

Novelist Paul Hemphill and his wife, Susan, will be in Tallahassee Friday night. Paul taught the writing class in which Grace and I met, and we became good friends. They moved from San Francisco to Atlanta during July.

Recently, I received a letter from Paul, saying, in effect, that I'm not yet ready to write a novel because I haven't "suffered" and struggled enough. He's really hung up on the suffering part. He enclosed an article he wrote for a weekly, talking about the divorce from his first wife. He's the same person I met two years ago, still writing about the same stuff. But I do like him, and he's a gifted writer, no question about it. By his own count, he has published 150 magazine articles and three books.

But I'm not about to determine my life's path based on his experiences. My novel might not be published for years. It might be revised several times. But now is the time to write it.

Grace wadded up Paul's letter and threw it across the room when I showed it to her. But I think what she read made her more sad than mad. Paul, she said, still hasn't gotten over his divorce, even though it was final almost two years ago. He hasn't been able to accept it and accept his feelings and move on, she added.

Sept. 8, Lake Ellen

I called Mindy tonight. She's a woman to whom I was engaged in college. I later broke the engagement when we just couldn't seem to get together geographically following graduation and my service in the military.

I hadn't talked to her in more than five years. My sister found out her phone number yesterday, called her, and then called me.

It was wonderful talking with her. It felt a lot like a movie plot, two old lovers learning each other's whereabouts after several years. I learned how cruel I had been to her over the phone, after I moved from Florida to Bucks County, Pa., back in 1971. I didn't remember the things I said. But she did.

"You do when you're on the receiving end," she said.

I told her something I haven't told anyone else, probably not even myself. I told her I thought I might have married Lois out of obligation, because that's what she wanted. Mindy said she thought it seemed a whirlwind affair.

I feel stimulated by our conversation. I probably won't sleep much tonight. I hope to get up to Duluth to see her when I go north this fall.

Mindy still sees a lot of her friends from college and knows a lot of the names of people who are still on the faculty at the Missouri Journalism School.

I haven't stayed in touch with anyone from school, and it bothers me a little. I've moved a lot since then. Am I running away from something? Or maybe to something? I hope it's the latter. I think I need to do some inner exploring, especially since I'm still drawn to Flat River. Where do I belong?

Maybe I'm most comfortable moving away from people and places, since that's what I've been doing all my life, even as a child. And maybe if I do move to Flat River, I'd soon want to move away again.

Mindy and I saw a musical called **Paint Your Wagon** when we were in college and a song called "Wand'rin' Star" was my favorite. Now maybe I better understand why:

> I was born under a wandrin' star.
> I was born under a wandrin' star.
> Wheels are made for rollin'.
> Mules are made to pack.
> I've never seen a sight that didn't look better looking back.

Sept. 9, Lake Ellen

I just talked to Grace and told her about my feelings of being lost and how it felt to talk with Mindy. She said I should start praying. Religion, she explained, is the act of putting purpose in your life. And praying, I guess, is what religion is all about.

I feel almost obligated to find all this talk about prayer and religion offensive. But I do not. Perhaps it's because I'm out here, alone and lonely (today, at least, and yesterday), and susceptible to such thoughts, such promises.

I don't think that's the reason, though. I think I don't find prayer and religion offensive right now because of the passionate and loving way Grace expressed her interpretations. I understood what she said. I felt what she said. And I didn't feel at all threatened or skeptical, as I do often around organized religion.

Prayer seems to be a way of letting out your innermost feelings, fears, wants, and needs. And it seems a way of acknowledging—to whom I do not know—your gratitude for life by expressing the joy, sorrow, confidence, or fear you feel at that moment. For most, prayer might be a way of keeping in touch with God, but it also seems a way of keeping in touch with yourself, of realizing who you are and why you are. Prayer also seems a celebration of life, any suffering that might be involved notwithstanding. Life is living, no more, no less, and certainly enough.

Sept. 18, Lake Ellen

A spectacular rainbow formed over the east end of the lake at sunset today. A faint second rainbow followed over the first. Colors from top to bottom: purple, pink, yellow, green, and blue.

For the second time this summer, some skiers tired to splash water on me as I stood fishing on the dock. Both times, they missed. This time, however, I responded. I retrieved my .22 rifle and propped it prominently on a rocking chair. They noticed, and didn't bother me again.

Doing something like that gave me a funny feeling inside, frightened, and, at the same time, exhilarated. The weapon wasn't loaded, and I didn't have ammunition with me.

Why do people enjoy trying to frighten or anger someone else? That includes me, as well as the skiers. We aren't really civilized, I think, and never will be. We're pretenders, frustrated both by what we are and what we are not.

Sept. 25, Lake Ellen

I saw Al English on Friday afternoon. Al is a street philosopher that I wrote an article about before I left the newspaper. And as happened with so many of my article subjects, we became friends.

Al is the first person who gave me hope for growing older. He's a self-proclaimed "optimistic pessimist." He's optimistic about Man on an individual basis, but not collectively.

He suffered a second heart attack a short while ago. He wasn't feeling well when I saw him. He also has emphysema, a hiatal hernia, and high blood pressure. And he's afraid.

Al has lots of friends, but he's alone most of the time in his little apartment. He probably will die alone, too, which I hope doesn't happen.

We talked a little about his dying. I said he would remain always with the many of us he has touched in Tallahassee. He wants me to take his "Notes to Myself" when he dies and see if I can get it published.

I told him I loved him and we both cried a little when I left.

Grace said it's a sin to not visit someone like Al. I told her how Al kept saying how wonderful it was to see me.

He also told me how hard it was not be depressed. He told me how he could put on a "front" for all the people who saw him on the street, but he couldn't keep it up when he was home alone.

What do you say to a very special person, someone who has made your life so much richer, who is dying? How do you comfort him? I wanted so much to say something profound and reassuring, but I couldn't find the words. Al would understand, though, and maybe laugh at the idea of a writer being without words. Life, he said, is a trage-comedy, and the best way to get through it is by laughing.

I'm going to see Al on a regular basis as soon as I get back into town. I told John yesterday that I want to move back in. I'll still work with him on his books, but I want to get a part-time job too.

I moved out here with the idea of working with John on a regular basis. But he hasn't been able to find the time to collaborate with me, and I can only do so much without his input. Then, I'm sitting out here alone.

The isolation was nice for three months. But I need to be around people now.

I've been spending quite a bit of time on my own writing, which is why I've been neglecting the journal, although, actually, this is my writing too, I guess. But I still have a lot of time on my hands out here, time I could be spending with others. I really look forward to being back in to civilization.

Sept. 30, Lake Ellen

Linda H. quit her job at the paper and invited me to dinner for a "victory celebration." A lot of others have quit too, since I left at the end of May. One called from a phone booth on the Pennsylvania Turnpike, and said he wasn't coming back.

I'm hoping Linda will do some features for the ***Flambeau***, the student newspaper at Florida State. Starting soon, I'm going to be both the consultant and features editor there for $350 a month. That's not a lot of money, but should be enough for me to get by.

Grace told me today about an old woman she met during a thunderstorm many years ago. The woman said she liked to take her umbrella and walk in the rain. She enjoyed being alone with her thoughts under the umbrella. And the storm, I guess, heightened the intensity of the moment.

Grace said she still thinks of that woman and feels gratified she was allowed to share such an intimate part of a stranger's life.

Part IV: My Neighbor Was a Serial Killer

Oct. 7, Lake Ellen

Tonight, I had one of those rare flirtatious experiences that leave me smiling for days. I was waiting with Beth to cross the street on the FSU campus. A car full of girls passed, and one of them looked at me almost (don't laugh) lustfully. I smiled and looked over at Beth, who half-smiled and seemed a little puzzled.

I broke the silence by mentioning I felt a little funny being on a college campus again and was wondering how old I looked.

"Getting looks like that, you don't have anything to worry about," she said.

The last time something like that happened was in Barcelona. This one was more enjoyable because someone else was around to see it, eliminating the possibility that I imagined the whole thing.

By the way, I worked with Beth at the ***Democrat***. She's an attractive young woman, and is one of the sweetest, most gentle people I know. I'm not sure why, but we've always been "just friends," as if by mutual, but unspoken consent.

I met Mike Sullivan's "old wife" at WFSU, the university radio station. She later asked me if I caught that description when she introduced herself. She said she wanted to be certain I knew she wasn't married anymore. She asked for my phone number. And I got hers.

Girls, girls, girls.

I went sailing Sunday with Gary and Ann, who brought along Carol Jones, a lawyer. I asked her to go to a party with me this Sunday. She said she couldn't because she would be out of town, "but I'd like to do something sometime."

Our sailing trip was exciting. Coming back from Dog Island, we had seas of five to six feet and winds of more than 25 knots. Ann and I had to climb up on the bow and, with life jackets on, cling to the side to keep the boat from heeling too much in the strong wind. We all got soaked and wind burned. It was Carol's first time sailing. Not a pleasant introduction for a beginner, I'm afraid. But, damn, being pummeled by the raw, rugged power of nature was an exhilarating experience!

Oh, yes, Becky has another girl for me to meet, Pam, a 23-year-old journalism student.

Oct. 14, Tallahassee

I moved back into town today. I'm living a couple of blocks from campus in a house that John owns and has turned into two apartments. I'm upstairs. I don't know yet who is downstairs.

Oct. 18, Tallahassee

So now, in the evenings, I'm hearing skateboards rattling down the street instead of frogs and crickets. But that's okay.

I was okay too when I woke up this morning to the sounds of a band marching through downtown.

John's girlfriend, Cathy, works with 3- and 4-year-old children who have speech problems. When it's time for them to be taken home, a teacher or assistant rides on the bus with them. One day, though, the bus driver left with only the children and a list with their names and addresses.

Several hours later, he returned to Easter Seal with all the kids. None of them could tell him their names or where they lived.

Cathy is another sweet soul. She and John, who's always in a hurry, seem an odd couple.

*****

At a party Saturday night, Jake Kraft told me some good ol' boy stories. He works for DOT, and sometimes his work takes him over to the small town of Chipley.

One of the stories was about "Nubsville," which is the nickname for an even smaller town, south of Chipley. It earned that name after an insurance fraud conspiracy was uncovered. People were shooting off fingers and toes to collect insurance.

The tip-off was that right-handed people were "accidentally" losing only fingers on the left hand. Also, a man who always drove a stick shift truck to work decided to drive an automatic the day he "accidentally" shot off a toe on his left foot.

Maybe I can work that into a short story.

Jake also was shown a place in the park where the "Martian" crashed. An Army veteran brought back a monkey with him to Chipley. When it died, he and some friends—their creative minds stimulated by a few six-packs—painted it blue, put it in the park, poured a circle of kerosene around it, and tossed a match. Voila! A flying saucer crash and Martian fatality.

*****

Well, Hell. Cathy's on my mind tonight, so I'll write more about her. I really like her, and I'm afraid that it's messing up my head. I lose sight of priorities.

And just what are my priorities? I feel insecure because I don't have a good-paying job anymore. Cathy is the kind of girl who always will have good, upper-middle class tastes and a desire to live well. And I guess I feel she would like me more if I were more conventional and a little wealthier.

There's no question I'd like to have more money and live better than I do. But I also want to be a writer and write what's important to me. Right now, I can see no way to have both.

Wow. That sounds so pompous. What, exactly, is important to me? I don't have a clue.

I told Beth that sometimes I'm not sure of who I am and where I belong. She gave me a very simple, very profound answer: In effect, make my own niche and don't feel I have to settle with one type of people with whom I'm comfortable or even two or three.

But I feel so helpless and somewhat worthless at the moment. I wouldn't even want a deep relationship with Cathy, even if she weren't John's girlfriend. Yet I'm attracted to her. I want, and I don't want at the same time. And I'm constantly dissatisfied.

I felt so anonymous walking across campus today. And I remembered how "good" I had it at the ***Democrat***, even though I wouldn't want to be there now. Watching the World Series, I remembered all of the good things about being a sports writer, before I moved over into features.

I miss my sports car too. I sold it when Sunny and I were planning to run away together. I've been thinking about that lately, too.

I'm living in an apartment that John owns and driving a car he owns. And that bothers me. I don't think it would so much if we could just get on with his book. But he hasn't been able to find the time during the past month.

I want so much to succeed as a writer. But will I? How many other thousands have wanted to and failed? Why can't there be some sort of test to gauge my capabilities? Why can't I find out if all my efforts will be wasted?

But, of course, they won't be. I want to write.

I also want to eat. Unfortunately, the two aren't necessarily mutually inclusive.

And I don't want to be "discovered" 10 years after my death. It really would piss me off not to be around when I'm a famous writer.

And that reminds me of another song, "Death of an Unpopular Poet," from Jimmy Buffett. Poor and mostly unsuccessful, the writer died, leaving his royalties to his dog. Then he became famous and rich, "and everybody wonders, did he really lose his mind? No, he was just a poet who lived before his time."

Oct. 23, Tallahassee

I've been depressed all day.

I saw Ellie for the second time last night. She cooked dinner here, and we spent the evening and morning (until 6:30 a.m.) talking and drinking wine.

Upon talking to her over the telephone for the first time, I had been hopeful of this relationship. She seemed so vibrant and alive. Our first date together, the Leon Thomas concert, was promising too.

But as last evening progressed, I grew sadder and sadder and more confused. Ellie drank the wine much more quickly than I and, as she did, stories emerged, some of them conflicting and many of them jaw-dropping.

She came from a wealthy family in North Dakota, she said. Then she talked about being poor. She was the sweetheart of Sigma Chi in college. She's had five abortions. She had a lump removed from one breast. She had pancreatitis. She was raped last April. She had a five-year relationship with a man in West Virginia. She left him five times.

She implied she had been in a mental institution. As she drank more and more, she seemed to lose awareness or pretended she did. She talked about a child who attends the school where she works. She seemed to drift in and out of reality, and I didn't know what to do or say.

When she was aware of where she was, she didn't make sense when she talked. Yet she was aware enough to know I was trying to placate her.

She seemed to object to the fact I was "in control" and she wanted me to drink more wine with her. She talked of working long, hard hours for minimum wage and then going home to take care of her niece for several hours each day.

She's living in a small apartment with her brother and his wife. She came from Denver in August, according to Grace, who works in the same building on campus with her sister-in-law. Yeah, that's how we got together—a fix-up.

Evidently, Ellie drinks wine to forget it all. She's really unhappy, I think, and she still feels a lot of resentment about her relationships with the man in West Virginia—if he even exists.

I want to call her again. I like her and am concerned about her. But I'm depressed and afraid about what might happen if we get together again. I don't know what to do.

Is this Sunny Sullivan all over again? A lot of motion without going anywhere? I'm beginning to think I'm fated to spend the rest of my life getting involved with women who have tragic stories. But is that their doing or mine? Mine, I'd say.

On the other hand, two in a row isn't exactly what I'd call a pattern of behavior. Still…

I saw Susan Friday night. But I don't want to do that again. It's too much of a strain. If I don't babble on and on, there are awkward silences. She's 28 or 29 and recently divorced. She's also not meeting anyone new, she said.

Oct. 26, Tallahassee

I saw Ellie last night. She said that she didn't remember a thing that happened after dinner on Saturday. I told her what she had said, and she confirmed it all.

I also asked her if she had done any drugs. "You name it," she said.

She hasn't been in a mental institution, but she has been in psychiatric wards. For my own peace of mind, at least, that seems a distinction without much difference.

I told her that she said her father once had said, "It's too bad you'll never be as pretty as your mother." She said it wasn't one time, but all the time. She said she had built a wall around herself.

Her brother and sister-in-law were very upset that she had stayed out all night. They were fearful for their reputations. If they only knew the sadness Ellie feels. Or maybe they do. But I'm doubtful.

She was talking of moving out. But I don't see how she can afford it. She works 30 hours a week at $2.30 an hour.

After having dinner with me last night, she was to go home and talk to her brother. She really was dreading it.

At lunch, I talked to Grace about the situation and my concerns. I also said that I felt as if I had tossed Ellie a life line and it wouldn't be right for me to pull it back, for fear of getting involved.

Grace told me I couldn't be Ellie's mother. People trying to be the world's mother is one of her favorite topics. She also told me about levels of misbehavior that are cries for help. Her daughter Linda is a classic case of Level One, which concerns attention-getting antics. Grace said my father is approaching Level Four, which is deep depression and an almost catatonic state.

She explained that direct response, such as acknowledging Linda's silliness, is the wrong approach. Instead, she helps meet Linda's need for attention by involving her in some activity, such as going shopping or cooking.

Grace said I should try to figure out what level Ellie is at and respond to her needs accordingly. I should have asked her how high the levels go.

From what I can discern, Ellie is very lonely and fearful of rejection—unless she's been drinking, which seems to be most of the time. Then sadness and anger come pouring out in stories about the slights, insults, and pain she has endured at the hands of others. I suspect that there's some truth in all of them. How much truth is the big question. Five abortions?

I called her this afternoon and she said that her meeting with her brother wasn't so bad after all. He apologized and gave her flowers, she said. She seemed really happy when I talked with her, and that made me feel better.

Grace also told me not to be fearful of trusting my feelings. She said she thought I still might have a few issues because of my ex-wife. "Garbage," she called them. She told me I shouldn't feel I had been rejected, sexually or emotionally, because I really hadn't. She also told me not to depend upon intellectual relationships, even though they are more non-threatening than emotional ties.

I told her that I'm beginning to fear I'm drawn to destructive relationships. She said if I were involved in a destructive relationship I would know it, because it was destructive. "That's not exactly reassuring," I replied.

Then she told me that she and Doug would tell me if they saw such a thing happening, just as I would tell them about what I felt.

I couldn't remember ever expressing feelings very forcefully to them, but she could. She mentioned my telling her she had better not cancel her doctor's appointment, as she had done before. She said that had irritated her a little, and I couldn't help laughing.

Nov. 7, Tallahassee

Ellie is mentally ill. If you are reading this, that might have been obvious to you before now. But I've had a difficult time coming to terms with that. I was so impressed by her in the beginning.

She knocked on my door Friday morning and said her brother Pete had kicked her out. She was staying at the nearby Holiday Inn. She wanted me to buy two bottles of wine for her, but I refused. She said she had only 11 cents left.

I took her to lunch and then for a walk at Maclay Gardens. She drank most of a bottle of wine when we got back to her room. She didn't want to leave the room again, or maybe she wanted to be coaxed. I coaxed and got her to go to dinner and a movie with me. While waiting for the movie, she popped down four capsules of some kind.

Back at her room, she started on the wine again. She said she needed it to help her think, to help her solve her problems. When she said, "I'm not drinking this fast enough," I decided to leave.

I told her it was too depressing for me to stick around. I told her I would see her the next day, and she said, "If I'm still alive."

She was still alive. The next day, she knocked on my door within five minutes of my return from the Mayfields. Ellie said she hadn't slept all night and wanted to take a nap. She told me not to pay any attention to her if she started crying or shaking. Yeah… right.

Later, she went to Pete's place and got some of her clothes. She was planning to stay with me for a few nights, I guess, until she found a place of her own. She said that she would say and do things that would shock me, but I wasn't to call the hospital, even if she asked me to call the hospital.

Through the evening, she talked more and more of suicide. I ignored her each time and talked about something else. As she opened a second bottle of wine, she told me that a liquor store gave the alcohol to her because "she was such a good customer."

I told her I was leaving. She said she wasn't going to drink anymore, and she put out her cigarette when I told her I was allergic to smoke.

Then she sat there, staring straight ahead. When she said, "I have to think about what I'm going to do," I finally gathered the courage to do what I knew I had to do—get out of there and find Ellie some help.

I went to the Mayfields and Grace suggested I call Pete. I did, and told him that Ellie was ill, I was not equipped to deal with her problems, and something needed to be done.

He and his wife Margie came over to the Mayfields and we talked. They hadn't seen Ellie for several years, they said, until she came down in August. They knew she had been having problems, but they weren't sure what they were. She seemed all right for about a month. Then the troubled behavior began.

She had expressed hatred of her father to me, I told them, and it seemed to me that she now was transferring that hatred to her brother, who was seven years older. Pete said he was afraid for both himself and his family. But, he said, he never told her to leave their home, although it seemed she was trying to provoke him into doing that.

Pete mentioned the hate he saw in her eyes. I saw it too, in a smoky, evil stare that I didn't know anyone was capable of. I saw it usually when Ellie had been drinking and was talking about her father, Pete, or Keith, the guy she said she left five times in West Virginia.

Pete said that he wasn't going to let her back in his apartment. And we decided I should tell her to leave my place. Actually, they decided. But the truth was that I probably was the only one she'd listen to so I had to be the one to do it.

I didn't go back that night, though. Instead, I lay sleepless on Grace's couch. And on Sunday morning, as I drove back to my place, I envisioned Ellie lying in a bloody pool in my bathroom. She had told me she cut her wrists once, and she did have scars on her right arm.

When I opened the door, Ellie seemed to be the person I was attracted to originally. There was no trace of the depressed and potentially suicidal person from the night before. But then I saw that self-destructive attitude return without pills or wine, and I was just as frightened as I was the day before. It was almost as if my arrival triggered it.

I told her I didn't know what was going on, but it made me unhappy and I didn't want to be involved in anything that made me unhappy. I had enough problems of my own, I said. I told her I hadn't slept and she seemed concerned. I didn't tell her I had talked to Pete and Margie.

Then she blamed Pete for me not sleeping and that blank stare in her eyes returned. "I'm sorry you didn't sleep," she said, as she carried her bag out of the apartment. Then she drove away.

It bothers me that I had to tell her to leave, even though I was miserable around her and knew it was necessary for my own safety and sanity. She'll find another place to go. She might be troubled, but I suspect that she's a master manipulator, at least with people who haven't known her for long, as I was. Still, though, my heart goes out to her. In that evil stare I see pain, unhappiness, and bewilderment.

Grace thinks Ellie might have taken a mind-altering drug that causes erratic behavior. Whatever the reason, Ellie needs help. I don't feel any emotional tie to her. Yet I grieve for her, and want to reach out. She's lost, and probably never will find her way back.

Grace also told me that Susan thinks very highly of me. Susan is one of several women that she has introduced me to this fall. I think highly of me too. Yet I also feel just the opposite. I feel people don't really know me and, if they did, they wouldn't think I'm so terrific. Still, it's not like I'm hiding anything about myself.

Frankly, I think the above paragraph is disgusting, and I'm going to jump off the thinking treadmill for tonight.

On Friday, I mailed a short story to **The New Yorker**.

Nov. 15, Tallahassee

Ellie called twice and someone knocked on my door at 1 a.m. Saturday morning. I didn't answer. She didn't say much on the phone, except to recount her bad fortune. I wanted to reach out, but I didn't. Ellie is the only person who can save Ellie. And, as Grace says, "You can't be the world's mother."

Thoughts on my feelings of loneliness and why it's really not so bad:

I haven't been still enough to find anyone. For more than a year and a half, starting with my separation from Lois, I've moved from one temporary situation to another. I can't find anyone by being continually on the move. I have to stop and look. I'm hoping that now I can stop and look.

Grace and Doug are responsible for the above realization.

Nov. 23, Tallahassee

One of the keys to breaking writing's block is realizing that you aren't going to write it right the first time. In fact, you might write it perfectly awful the first time. But it gets better, maybe even good, and that's what is important. You just have to start.

Beth is going to work for the **New York Times**. Her father got her a job editing and transmitting wire copy. I'm really happy for her, but I will miss her.

Nov. 25, Tallahassee

Fifteen years ago, Grace, the girls, and her former husband, Jim, lived in Ohio, next to poet John Crowe Ransom. Karen played leap frog with Ransom and Aldous Huxley, Grace said. He was very tall, she remembered, while Ransom was small. The latter was dressed in a coat and tie, and Huxley in a beige shirt and trousers. They made a striking contrast.

Nov. 30, Tallahassee

I haven't written in too long a time. Mental and emotional exhaustion from dealing with Ellie had something to do with that, I suppose. But recently, I have managed to send out another short story and an article about procrastination to a business magazine.

There's some irony, I think.

Also, I just finished taking a two-night class about keeping a saltwater aquarium. It was rather a disappointment. The teacher knew the topic, but knowing it isn't enough. Mastery of the subject doesn't mean you have the ability to share what you know in a way your students will understand.

That reminds me of journalism. Journalists must have both the knowledge and the ability to share so readers can learn and understand.

Maybe that sounds condescending. But that's all right. I feel condescending when it comes to much of the world.

*****

Ellie stopped by on Friday. Fortunately, a friend was here, and we were just leaving. She said she was looking for a lawyer because her brother was trying to take away her inheritance.

She still has her job, which she told me some time ago that she was afraid of losing. Doug told me that she might have "lost" it if I offered her comfort and assistance. I think he's right.

I haven't been with a woman since Ellie. Nor have I felt the desire to initiate relationships with any.

I've really met some crazies since last spring. Donna was the first, while I was still at the newspaper and before I met Sunny. She and her husband are artists, and I interviewed them in their home for a feature. We hit it off really well, I stayed for dinner, and, seemingly in a flash, it was midnight. Donna's husband went to bed, but she wanted me to stay and talk some more. I did.

Finally, at dawn, she walked me to my car. It was a gorgeous spring morning, with birds singing and a heavy dew sparkling on flowers and trees. Donna broke off a rose, gave it to me, and kissed me on the cheek.

I didn't see her again. Not long after, she called, told me that she loved me, and said she was leaving town. I haven't heard from her since.

Then there was Sunny, a lot of motion going nowhere and a great strain on my health, since I still was recovering from mono during our tempestuous (I've always wanted to use that word!) relationship.

And the latest: Ellie the ill.

Aren't there any stable ones out there? Sure, there are. And, in time, the right one will come along.

Actually, I like living alone. Except when I'm lonely.

Oh, yes, I don't usually remember much from dreams. But this morning I awoke and remembered something about 9 ½ inches of snow falling in St. Louis and "we have copious quantities of cream here in the Creole." I don't think I'll ever figure out that one.

*****

Dec. 5, Tallahassee

Ellie stopped by again last night, and I made the mistake of letting her in. Earlier in the day, she left a message saying "I've learned a lot lately." If she had, she didn't show it. She marched into my apartment with her few possessions, accused her brother of raping her, and announced that she was staying.

I told her that she couldn't do that and, in response, she locked herself in the bathroom. The first thing that I felt was relief that I had nothing in there that she could hurt herself with. I use an electric razor. And the shower curtain could not support her weight if she tried to hang herself.

But almost certainly she had pills with her.

And then it hit me. Maybe she had a straight razor too. Or a knife. Or gun.

This situation quickly had evolved into something that I was not equipped to deal with. Before, I had asked her to leave and she did. That was not going to be the case this time.

I drove to the Mayfields and, with Grace's support, called Ellie's brother. I told him what had happened and that he was going to have to deal with this. He said that he would.

Dec. 14, Flat River, Mo.

That's right. I'm home for the holidays again. What happened with Ellie wasn't the only reason that I decided to leave Tallahassee for awhile, but it was a big part of it.

I don't know specifically who took Ellie out of my apartment. Maybe Pete was able to do it himself. Maybe he had to have help from the police.

But I do know that she was in the hospital the next day. A couple of days after that, I took her flowers and wished her the best. She didn't look well and was barely responsive.

The doctors said that when she was admitted, she was so high on drugs that she probably didn't remember anything from the past week or so. Maybe she didn't even remember me.

As I left the hospital, I felt so bad for her and the role that I had played in possibly enabling her to continue her life of self-destruction. Later, Grace reminded me again that I can't be the world's mother—or Ellie's either.

What I've come to realize is that we always will experience emotional ups and downs. They're part of the human experience. They're what it means to be alive. We err when we put too much emphasis on our reasons for being sad or even happy.

True, those reasons might be valid. But if they weren't present, we'd find others to rationalize what we're feeling. We need those reasons to put order in our lives and make sense of it.

The bottom line is that we are alive, and that is enough.

*****

In other news, Michael Musto still has not begun filming his movie, **Hank**. More and more I suspect that he will not, although I'm not sure why. But, he said, he is forming a theatrical company and will present musicals in Tallahassee next year.

*****

Here in small-town Missouri, meanwhile, the big news is that the wife of a prominent businessman discovered he was cheating on her. She waited until he was asleep and then glued his penis to his leg. That's according to my mother, who added that he wasn't circumcised and, consequently, "was in bad shape."

"He couldn't even go to the bathroom," Mom said. "They weren't even sure he was gonna live for awhile. She would have been tried for manslaughter.

"It's the truth," she continued. "Dad came home and told it. Virginia down at the store had heard about it. And yesterday over at the beauty supply place, someone started talking about it. It really did happen. He was in the hospital."

*****

Mom also revealed that Clay, my favorite uncle, just got married for the fourth time and moved to Tijuana from San Diego. She's not at all happy about that and suspects foul motives by the Mexican woman he married.

*****

I'm always hopeful when I come back home, but then reality slaps me in the face. When will I learn? Things don't change here.

But why should they? To meet my expectations?

I grew up receiving only criticism, never encouragement, especially from my father. On the plus side, I'm impressed I was able to endure here for so long. But at what cost?

I still can't be myself here. I quickly slide from hopeful to resignation and retreat into my shell and endure.

I'd like to spend as much time as possible away from home while I'm home, visiting with friends.

Dec. 15, Flat River

I spent some time with Mike B. today. As teens, we went fishing and played softball and football together.

People often remember you by the incidents you forgot. Mike said that he never will forget the football game when everyone but me wore boots and galoshes because of the mud and snow. I wore "tennis shoes with baggies around them and outran everybody," he recalled.

Mike is a loan officer. For the first time in his career, he lost his temper the other day when a woman said that she couldn't make a payment because she couldn't "shit money."

He said that he then called her a syphilitic old woman. He also said that if she didn't pay he would come out and take her furniture, car, carpeting, and "the ceiling."

She later called back to ask how he could take the ceiling and thanked Mike for the "opportunity to pay on the loan."

He said that she really is a "syphilitic old whore," but was shocked that he called her that aloud.

Mike and his wife just bought a house. He said that having a house, children, and a job he's happy with are what's important in his life. He didn't say it defensively either. And he acknowledged that not everyone wants that. He really seemed content. Good for him.

Dec. 18, Flat River

Full many a gem of purest ray serene
The dark unfathom'd caves of ocean bear:
Full many a flower is born to blush unseen,
And waste its sweetness on the desert air.
—Thomas Gray, excerpt from Elegy in a Country Churchyard

Dec. 22, Flat River

And here we go…

Mom just told me about the 16-year-old daughter of some friends who had "a half-Negro baby."

She wanted to get an abortion," she said. "But they wouldn't let her. I think it would have been better for the baby."

"A half-Negro," she believes, wouldn't fit in. "He won't have anything to do with Negroes," she said. "And white people won't have anything to do with him."

Of course, I couldn't keep my mouth shut. "Not everybody is that way," I said.

"Would you want your daughter marrying a half-Negro boy?" she asked.

"If she wanted to," I said. "It would be her decision, and I certainly wouldn't have a problem with it."

"Well, I would," she replied.

Of course, I was spitting in the wind, but I continued. I told her that people with those kinds of attitudes were the ones that would make it tough for the child. And I used the word "prejudiced."

"I don't think that I'm any better than they are," she said. "I'll stay in my place, and they should stay in theirs. And I don't want my daughter marrying one."

My mother's "place" is about the smallest I've seen, and her barriers of inflexibility grow higher and higher as she gets older.

*****

We visited my grandparents today. Their house is filled with religious books, including ***Day-by-Day*** by Billy Graham, and key chains. The latter, from all over the country, were brought to them by the children, grandchildren, and great grandchildren in all those pictures that cover the walls.

Craig put a new seat on their toilet. The old one was 36 years old, and put on when the house was built. MamMa said she had tried to get PapPa to put on a new one, but he said the old one "will outlast both of us."

MamMa showed me my grandfather's pocket watch. It's 57 years old. In 1920, she sold a sow and seven pigs for $100 and bought the watch for $45. They were going to the oil fields in Texas, she said, and he needed a watch.

Dec. 30, Flat River

I spent a couple of days with my friends, Dave and Shirley, in Chicago. We saw Hemingway's birthplace and Frank Lloyd Wright's home. Next to Wright's home is a house with red, plastic flowers sticking up through the snow. I can't help wondering how old Frank would feel about that.

We ate at a Russian restaurant and a combination "pizzeria and Mexican fiesta."

David told a lot of funny stories. He went through one Little League season without getting a base hit and finished 0-91, all strikeouts. He showed me a scar on his knuckle, the result of a nun hitting him with a metal ruler when he was in Catholic elementary school.

Lois and I became friends with them about four years ago in graduate school at Central Missouri State. But they seem to have become "my friends" since the divorce. That's okay with me. They're great people, funny and full of life, and we have a good time together.

*****

Craig is working nights as a desk clerk at a local motel. He showed me some of the literature left in rooms, including **Tight Bondage** and **In Daddy's**

Arms. In one room, someone put a poster of the Dallas Cowboy Cheerleaders on the wall.

He said that local people often try to rent rooms, which is against motel policy. When they're turned down, they often threaten and argue.

It's easy to tell a "shack-up," he said, because the man always parks the car out of sight and comes in alone to rent a room. One night, he said, six or seven local people tried to rent rooms.

Jan. 15, 1978, Tallahassee

Sirens jolted me awake in the darkness of this early Sunday morning. It sounded like they were right outside my door. My upstairs apartment doesn't have windows facing the street, so I couldn't see anything.

Was the house on fire? Or a neighboring house? I couldn't smell smoke. I stepped outside and saw flashing lights to the right, between my apartment and the FSU campus. They appeared to be in front of a sorority house, but I wasn't curious enough to get dressed and go check it out.

This afternoon, I learned what happened and met my neighbors for the first time. I answered a knock to see two girls standing there with a baseball bat.

They gave me their names, Sandy and Ellen, and told me they live downstairs. "We were thinking that we need to look out for each other after what happened at the Chi Omega house last night," Ellen said.

I told them that I heard the sirens but didn't know what happened.

"Two girls were killed and maybe more. We don't know for sure," she explained. "It was awful.

"Everybody is scared. Some of my friends said that they're going home."

I felt a chill roll down my spine. A little more than a block away, college girls had been murdered, probably while they were asleep in their beds.

"Oh, my God," I said. "That's awful."

I gave them my name and agreed that we should look out for each other. We also exchanged phone numbers.

After I closed the door, I pulled my .22 rifle out of the closet, made sure it was loaded, and then leaned it in a corner, within reach from the bed.

Also, I remembered when I had gone up to Columbia, Mo., years before to take an entrance exam for Journalism School at the University of Missouri. That same day, the paper reported the murder of a young couple in their home. Initially, the idea of living in a town where such things happened frightened me. But eventually I just chalked up the fear to being more about leaving the security of home than real danger to me. After all, awful things like that happen everywhere, I reasoned.

And another one had just occurred in Tallahassee, Fla.

*****

When I returned from Missouri, Grace told me that Ellie left Tallahassee. I hope that she has the strength to overcome her demons.

First I got involved with Sunny and then Ellie. I really have to question my judgment. No more relationships for awhile, please. Not even any blind dates. I must remember to tell Grace, my enthusiastic matchmaker.

And enough with writing about writing in this journal. I'm writing short stories, essays, and time management articles, and trying to sell them. I'm writing features and reviews for the **Flambeau**. I am not working on the novel. I am not working on the mayfly book, primarily because John can't find the time to help. And I'm okay with all of that.

And enough with writing about relationships too!

Jan. 16, Tallahassee

It was awful.

The Tallahassee Democrat devoted a full page today to the atrocities that occurred Saturday night. And it wasn't just at the Chi Omega house either, although that's where the worst of it happened.

This monster killed two at the sorority and almost killed two more. I suspect that he was frightened by something, maybe a noise, and fled before he could finish. He beat and strangled his victims, as well as possibly raped them.

He then ran six blocks and broke into a house, attacking another girl with a board. She's in critical condition with a fractured skull, according to the paper.

The town's population is in shock, while those on and near the FSU campus are absolutely traumatized. University officials visited dorms and sororities with the specific intent to "put the fear of the Lord into you." They advised girls to go outside only with guys. They told them to report anyone who is "weird, strange, or creepy."

At the **Flambeau** offices, I heard gossip about quite a few students thinking about dropping out and going home for the rest of the semester.

The Democrat is offering a $2,500 reward for the arrest and conviction of the murderer.

Intellectually, it's difficult to fathom that pure evil exists in the world. But then something like this happens in your little part of the world, and you have no doubt.

*****

Earlier this month, I had an accident in one of John's junkers. Someone ran a red light and slammed into me as I made a left turn into a parking lot. Fortunately, I wasn't injured.

A few days later, the brakes went out on another. Then the transmission puked in a third, about two weeks after the water pump broke. Someone is trying to tell me something.

In February or March, I'm going to fly up to Missouri for a short visit and to buy a used car. I'm pretty sure I can get a good deal up there, since my father is the business manager of a dealership. And I think the time has come for me to start thinking about having a little more permanence and stability in my life—like my own means of transportation. It's been more than a year since I had my European adventure.

Jan. 22, Tallahassee

Yes, some students—mostly girls, I suspect—have left FSU for the remainder of the term. On and around campus, everyone remains on high alert. Guys sleep in the lobbies and halls of girls' dorms to protect their friends. They walk with them to and from classes, especially those later in the day.

One girl told me that many don't even go to the bathroom alone and they sleep with the lights on. Many, like those in the apartment below me, sleep with baseball bats by their sides. And they intently watch local news on TV and listen on the radio, hoping to hear that the monster has been caught.

In regard to the news, I do the same.

*****

I've been fighting a cold or virus of some kind for a couple of weeks. Doctor gave me something called Actifed, and it knocked me on my butt! It made me so light-headed that I could hardly walk. I've never taken drugs so I don't know what getting "high" feels like. But if it's like what I experienced, I don't want any part of it.

Feb. 1, Tallahassee

Based on the little I knew about what happened to her when she was a child, I didn't bring up the subject of the sorority murders to Grace. And neither did she, Doug, or the girls when I was around.

But yesterday, as we were chatting on her front porch during a warm winter's day, I learned that she probably was thinking about it. Suddenly, Grace stopped talking, and stared down the street. My eyes followed hers and I saw the headless child-size torso of a doll lying atop a garbage can in front of a neighbor's house.

Suddenly, she started speaking again. But it wasn't small talk as it had been before. It was about the deranged elementary school teacher who had taken her and two friends out into a rural area, assaulted and tortured them, and left them for dead.

At times, she said, she still feels guilt that he did kill one of them.

He took them to a clump of trees to "show them the view." He then raped, cut, and brutalized them, she revealed, laughing as he did so.

He left them for a moment and told them not to scream.

"Emily didn't have an arm. I still can remember trying to put it back on her," Grace said. "That guilt has stayed with me too. I learned that when I went through therapy. It's something I have to live with."

Grace also screamed. But when the teacher asked who screamed, she denied it. Emily didn't say anything. Most likely, she already was dead.

"Her eyes were open," Grace said.

But the teacher did some more cutting and beating on Emily, and Grace feels remorse about that as well.

Grace has scars all over her body from the ordeal. The teacher, she said, tried to carve words or symbols on their bodies. She often feels ugly and ashamed. And having four beautiful daughters, she revealed, sometimes heightens her feelings of inadequacy.

The girls know nothing of what happened to her. Grace said that she has told only me and the psychiatrist such a detailed and intense account of the incident. Evidently, Doug learned the basics during much less emotional moments.

The scar tissue Grace has from the attack and her several operations possibly will be the death of her, she fears. She has lumps in her breasts and under her arms.

And what did I say in response as Grace told me these things? What could I say? All I could do was inadequately express my sorrow and tell her how much I care for her and the girls.

I am so saddened by what happened to her, as well as the realization that the three who survived their brutal beatings two weeks ago likely will suffer as Grace has suffered in the years to come.

Feb. 17, Tallahassee

I can't believe it! I just saw photos of the murder suspect in the **Pensacola News**, and I remember seeing him several times in the area where I live. He was riding a bike.

And that suggests he could have been my neighbor—a psychotic killer living downstairs, next door, or across the street.

The headline with the photos and story says, "Mystery Man Denied Bond," with a subhead of "FSU Link Sought."

As the headline suggests, he hasn't yet been identified. He was stopped and arrested near Pensacola because the orange VW Beetle that he was driving was reported stolen.

He's a good-looking guy, not the type you'd suspect of being a brutal murderer. But knowing that he might be, I think his smile in one of the photos is really creepy.

I hope this is the guy, and I'm sure that thousands of college students, their parents, and the Tallahassee community in general hope so as well.

Feb. 24, Tallahassee

Ted Bundy!

That's the name of the guy arrested in a stolen car in Pensacola and almost certainly the monster who murdered two girls and brutalized three others. Police found IDs from three FSU female students and 21 stolen credit cards in the car. He's now in jail here in Tallahassee.

And I wasn't the only one who saw him around here either. Witnesses have come forward to help tie him to the Chi Omega murders.

He's wanted nationally too. While awaiting trial for murder in Colorado last year, he escaped, and I'm guessing that's what put him on the FBI's Top Ten Fugitives list.

The killer might be in custody, but the nightmare never will be over for the survivors and the families of the victims. Grace's experience really has brought home to me how profound the suffering can be. I feel so sorry for them.

March 9, Tallahassee

I'm updating my address book tonight. Crossing through names always have given me a strange feeling. By Xing them out, I almost feel a murderer. Marking through their names means I have decided to remove those people from my life entirely.

*****

After 10 years, I finally have realized girls almost always say the same thing after you have kissed them good night: "Drive carefully."

March 15, Tallahassee

Police have found an FSU van that Bundy stole after the Chi Omega murders. It contains evidence linking him not only to that crime, but to the abduction of a 12-year-old girl in Lake City, who is still missing. Tragically, almost certainly she is dead.

March 23, Tallahassee

I'm back from Flat River with a used 1971 yellow Ford Maverick. It's not exactly a luxury vehicle. But it should be safer and more reliable than John's stable of clunkers.

*****

My Uncle Clay is in the hospital in San Diego. He's in serious condition with pneumonia and a fractured hip. He's lost 60 pounds in the past year, and, to my knowledge, he's never weighed more than about 150. I can't imagine what he must look like.

More than a year ago, we also learned that he had a degenerative brain disease.

Clay, my mother's older brother, is my favorite uncle. Heck, he's my favorite relative. Period.

When I was a teen and he would come visit from California during the summer, we'd play tennis. And at night, lying in adjoining beds and listening to the crickets just outside the open windows, we'd talk about books and authors and the St. Louis Cardinals.

As a Christmas present, he gave me a subscription to *The Saturday Review*. He revealed that he had corresponded with Norman Mailer and that he had sold a few short pieces to magazines—and failed to sell many more.

While serving on a bomber crew over the Pacific during World War II, he was wounded by anti-aircraft and received the Purple Heart, as well as other medals. After the war, he married a woman whose family owned a roadhouse in Alaska. While living up there, he shot a Kodiak bear.

They had one child, Cam, who died in childbirth when she was 19. I don't think that Clay ever has fully recovered from that. After his divorce, he worked at a variety of jobs, including as a teacher. I guess I view him as a tragic, but heroic figure. Others in the family likely consider him the black sheep for his unorthodox lifestyle. That's an honor I just might assume one day, I suspect.

I last saw him a couple of years ago, and we talked about me coming out to visit him in San Diego. I really wanted to do that, but procrastinated. Now, it's probably too late. I can't tell you how much I regret failing to do that.

He was living in Tijuana with a woman and her children. "Mexicans," my mother calls them in a derogatory voice, as if they are something less than human. She claims the doctors said he should have been brought into the hospital much sooner. She blames the woman for that not happening.

Mom told me previously that this woman was Clay's fourth wife. Now she's not so certain that they are married. She concerned about getting his "insurance papers and personal things" from "them" when she flies out there soon.

Billie, Clay's third wife, has been providing my mother with progress reports. She said Clay responded to some questions. And he drank chocolate milk.

Adding to Mom's stress, my father has been having headaches and double vision, but doctors can find no cause.

And her little dog, Mitzi, died in her sleep. She was a 10-year-old Peek-a-Poo that my sister left behind when she got married.

*****

While I was in Flat River, I learned that Kelly is married—again. That didn't take long.

I also learned that my parents still are playing the same game that they were when I was in Flat River for Christmas in 1976. Hero, the dog next door, continues to wake the neighborhood every morning at 6 with incessant barking, and they continue to complain every night at supper, but never do anything about it.

I was tempted to tell the neighbors to keep their dog quiet. But this little intrigue has been going on for so long, I can't bring myself to destroy the fun. My parents hate Hero, but they obviously hate him only enough to add passion to their own lives. Shutting him up would still the passion—and supper conversation.

Besides, if I were to tell Mom that I was going to do that, she would say," Oh, Robert, you can't do that.

Those are our neighbors. We have to live next door to them."

When I was growing up, one of her favorite sayings to me was "Oh, Robert, that could be dangerous."

*****

I got two blisters on my fingers the other day, winding my self-winding watch.

March 24, Tallahassee

What you gain as you grow older isn't nearly as important as what you refuse to lose.

April 2, Tallahassee

Authorities have found the body of the 12-year-old girl that Bundy abducted from Lake City. It was discovered near Suwannee River State Park. She was raped and her throat cut.

Now knowing how Grace has suffered for decades after what she saw and survived, I feel so sorry for the family, friends, and teachers of this poor child.

*****

My mother called tonight, after getting back from San Diego. Uncle Clay is expected to die soon and she will go back because "you can't have a funeral and not have anybody there."

She spent all day and night with Clay, every day she was there, she said. She had to wear a surgical mask because of a possibility that Clay has a virus of some sort. He also might have brain cancer. My mother said the doctor told her that Clay had suffered blows to both the front and back of his head.

He was married on Feb. 11 and taken to the hospital on March 4. Mom didn't learn he was in the hospital until weeks later. There now is talk that the blows might have been intentional, instead of from a fall. But why, then, would the family take him to the hospital?

My mother thinks his wife married him to get his pension. She has all of his papers at her home in Tijuana.

Although Mom couldn't see it, a nurse told her that Clay smiled when he first saw her. She talked to him about me, Craig, Rhonda, and his brother, Frank, and playing tennis. As she did, she said, "a tear came to the corner of his eye." He's on pain killers 24 hours a day and he sleeps in a straight jacket.

The nurse warned Mom that he might bite and scratch. He's fed through his nose. And former wife Billie said that, at times, he raises his hands and shouts, "Oh, God! Oh, God!"

Mom also visited the cemetery, where he is to be buried next to his daughter. She said, "It's a really pretty cemetery."

And, incredibly, for the first time, she told me that Clay had another daughter, Mary Louise, who is in a "convalescent home."

That trip, I think, probably was the toughest thing my mother has ever had to do. I admire her for it.

April 12, Tallahassee

Answering service: "Yes, sir you have a message. It's about your Uncle Clay… He died."

When she couldn't reach me, Mom left a message I later discovered, because she was leaving immediately for California.

May 9, Tallahassee

John and Cathy broke up. I can't say that I'm surprised. He's a good guy and very generous—except with his time. Since he's a time management expert, that, of course, is the ultimate irony.

Although I've managed to collect enough information from him to write magazine articles on topics like procrastination and delegation, I doubt that we'll ever do a book.

*****

Why is it we can recognize the important things in life, but then refuse to act on them? Taking the time to visit my Uncle Clay in San Diego comes to mind. I feel so awful about my failure to do that.

*****

Mom told me last night that Craig is engaged. He's known the girl about two months. They have the same birth day, month, and year. The wedding is set for April 6 of next year.

*****

To a Butterfly Aflutter:
Notice now the new flowers.
Not all will be sweet.
Yet one will be sweeter.

My poem is bad.
My rhyme will be worse.
So give me a smile,
Or I'll give you a verse.

May 29, Tallahassee

The toughest part of reaching for a star is suffering the comments of all those frustrated spectators who are afraid to do anything but criticize. They'll never realize that the star provides little more than direction.

The reaching is everything, a celebration of life, enjoying, enduring, truly living, despite, or possibly even because of, the voices of all the critics.

June 3, Tallahassee

I had a great time Thursday night—and Friday morning—after the play. Six of us went dancing at the Seafox. When it closed at 2 a.m., we then went to Mary's house on Lake Bradford and someone suggested we go swimming.

I'm reasonably certain that alcohol intake played a role in our decision to do just that in a lake full of alligators under a full moon.

Hand in hand, Mary and I walked with the rest through the live oaks and Spanish moss down to the dock. Someone had brought a radio and he turned to a rock and roll station and pumped up the volume. I don't remember the song. It was something by Fleetwood Mac.

We dropped our clothes and plunged in. Yikes! Yes, it's June, but that water was cold!

At least our shrieks probably scared away the gators.

Or did they? Something brushed my leg. I'd like to think it was Mary, but I don't know. I do know that she smiled at me and then swam into the shadows. I followed. And that's all I'm going to say about that.

Oh, okay, nothing happened except a little kissing. I still don't know about her marital status and that made me hold back, even though she might have been willing or even eager to do more.

Mary is British and Greek, and Grace introduced us at Mike Musto's production of ***No, No, Nanette!*** She's from London and came to the U.S. about five years ago. She used to work for WFSU-TV. Now's she's an actress and director, doing graduate work. She's directing ***Fortune and Men's Eyes***, a play that I've been helping with backstage and as an extra.

And yes, I got involved in the production because I'm attracted to her, especially her red hair and British accent. She hasn't revealed much about her recent past, but she has made occasional references to her relationship with a "friend" in the Tampa area, and, based on what I've heard during weeks of rehearsals, he's probably more than that. Maybe he's a husband and they're separated. Maybe he's an ex-husband. I've also heard that he's black and in prison. Boy, can I pick 'em!

Jennie, George, Tom, and Laura also were with us Thursday night. Jennie is the assistant stage manager for the play. Tom has one of the leads. George is the hairdresser. He has a small gold earring and a well-trimmed beard and wears Christian Dior shirts. I don't think he would be reluctant to admit he's homosexual. He's planning a trip to California soon.

In fact, I suspect that all of the men in the play are gay as well. That's appropriate, I guess, since the play is about homosexuality in prison. One character's name is "Queenie" and the guy who plays him fits that gay stereotype perfectly. And he does so proudly.

Laura is a costumer and a fashion plate. She also possesses a tongue capable of achieving extraordinary velocities. She's seems naturally theatrical with a good sense of humor. She reminds me of Annie Hall from the Woody Allen movie.

Although it hasn't worked out with Mary the way I initially hoped it would, I have to say that I've really enjoyed working with and socializing with these people. For a small town boy from Missouri, they seem larger than life.

June 6, Tallahassee

On the play's final night, Mary played host to a cast party at her house, and I celebrated by getting stoned. Well, actually, that's not true. I got stoned—my first time ever. Just not intentionally.

But let's start with earlier in the evening.

We were eating, drinking, laughing, and generally having a good time when two strangers arrived who decidedly were not theater types. Actually, they weren't strangers to Mary. They were friends of her husband, who, yes, is black and, yes, is in prison. Their tattoos suggested that they might have done time too.

They weren't interested in socializing either. They spoke quietly to Mary for a bit. Then they sat down at a table with a ***Playboy Magazine*** and a one-dollar bill. As one of them rolled the bill into a small tube, the other produced a bag of white powder. With the powder poured on the magazine cover, they then took turns snorting it.

The rest of us pretended not to notice, as we drank and talked in small groups. Or maybe I was the only one pretending. Maybe everyone else had seen guys do cocaine plenty of times—or even snorted it themselves. But for me, it was a first.

Fortunately, they didn't stay long. And I am certain when I say that the mood significantly brightened when they were gone. Then Mary produced a tray of brownies. Oh, boy, I love brownies!

I ate one and then another. Mary told me that I should slow down since they were laced with marijuana—another first for me. But I wasn't feeling anything unusual so I told her that they weren't having any effect.

And they didn't, until all at once they did. Suddenly a bowling ball was rolling around loose in my head. As I tilted to one side, the ball slid that way and pressed my head down to my shoulder. When I raised it up with both hands and considerable effort, the ball rolled the other way and pushed my head down on the opposite side.

Staggering and bouncing off furniture, I carried my head over to the sofa and sat down. I think that someone laughed and I laughed back. Finally, I decided to stop fighting the weight and let my head rest on the sofa arm. After that, I just sort of zoned out. I think that Mary and the gang could have stripped me naked and rolled me over a cactus and I wouldn't have felt a thing.

When I finally awoke, the bowling ball seemed to have fallen out of my ear and I could raise my head again. For a change, feeling "light-headed" was a good thing!

As I gobbled up a bowl of pretzels, I noticed that everyone else had left sometime during my drug-induced nap. My watch read almost 3 a.m.

"Well, I guess I'd better go," I said as I started for the door.

"Are you sure you can drive?" Mary asked.

I laughed. "Yeah, no problem," I said. "I'm more embarrassed than anything."

Mary laughed too. "Well, I did warn you," she replied.

"Next time, I'll listen," I said, only I knew there wouldn't be a next time for Mary and me.

She smiled and we lightly kissed goodnight. "Good night. It's been fun," I said before turning and heading for my car.

It was too—mostly. But as I sit here and write this, I'm thinking, "Sunny, Ellie, Mary… Boy, can I pick 'em!"

Yeah, I know. I've said that before.

June 7, Tallahassee

After dinner tonight at the Mayfields, Mike Musto talked about Jayne Mansfield. He said that he was her manager for seven years. He said he was producing her first full-length dramatic role, **Single Room Furnished**, when she was killed in a car accident on June 29, 1967.

She died three days before her divorce was to be final. Thus, her third husband inherited much of her estate, instead of nothing. I think that his name was Matt.

Mike said she was extremely intelligent and spoke seven languages. But she was "dumb about men."

At age 14, she married Jack Mansfield. When he was graduated from high school, they moved from Texas to California, where he attended UCLA. Jayne had a baby. When he finished college, he returned to Texas. She did not.

Several years later, she married a guy named Mickey as a publicity stunt. Mickey had been one of

Mae West's "studs," receiving $300 a week and more for his services.

Mae called Jayne a drunk and a whore when Mike suggested Jayne as the star for ***The Mae West Story***. Mae's maid heard everything and, after being fired, she went to work for Jayne, and told her.

Jayne decided to get even. She hired Mickey for $500 week and gave him a five-year guarantee. Mae hired a hit man to get Mickey, so he and Jayne left the country.

Mike said that Mae had "four musclemen" living with her when she criticized Jayne. He said Jayne "drank only socially" and was not a whore.

And, for dessert, Mike shared a juicy tidbit about Elizabeth Taylor. He said she has "piano legs," which is why her lower anatomy never received much exposure.

In the past, he's also talked about others. He said that he was Humphrey Bogart's script advisor for three years. He said that he hung out with John Steinbeck and Bill (William) Saroyan.

Over time I've started to develop doubts about the authenticity of Musto's plans for Rachel and, by extension, I've begun to wonder just how much he says about his career is true. Throw my experience with the daughter of a Hollywood actor into the mix, and I can't help but question the dependability and honesty of people in the entertainment world.

Still, the "insider" information he shared tonight was compelling. And even if it was not 100 percent true, it was thoroughly entertaining.

June 16, Tallahassee

It was Grace's turn tonight to regale me with stories from her past. Doug had something to do related to his pharmacy classes at FSU. So, after dinner, the two of us sat out on the front porch, enjoying the sunset, as she opened up.

The topic was Jim Olson, her brilliant, but now mentally ill former husband.

One morning, the girls went into breakfast and saw that he had dyed their cream of wheat. "And not any pale or pastel color either," Grace said. "Some of it was royal blue. Some of it was deep purple…"

Jim learned Portuguese by listening to short wave radio.

On their wedding night, he was entertained by filling his pants' pockets with rice, hanging them upside down, and listening to the rice fall to the floor. He did that twice.

Grace met Jim in a psychiatric ward. She was a patient. He was not. Considering what happened during their subsequent marriage, there's more than a little irony there, I guess.

She had just become Episcopalian and a psychologist had suggested she was a "latent homosexual" on the basis of a 10-minute test. As a consequence, she was admitted to a Baptist hospital. I asked if the hospital was supposed to cure her of being Episcopalian or homosexual.

June 24, Tallahassee

Doug and I talked about commuting tonight. He's finishing up at pharmacy school and looking for a job. I told him how hard I thought it would be to drive long distances back and forth every day. He said people get used to bad habits.

I said one of man's biggest bad habits is that he gets used to bad habits.

June 28, Tallahassee

Oh, boy, more entertainment industry stories from Mike.

Theatrical producer Lee Shubert told him a producer is a bum if he isn't sued at least 50 times a year. Shubert hit 1,000 one year. Samuel Goldwyn 1,700. Goldwyn also bankrupted seven corporations.

Mike said Goldwyn was a real "goniff." He would refuse to pay bills and then get creditors to accept 20 cents on the dollar instead of enduring two or three years of lawsuits to get it all. Then he would convince those same creditors to do business with him again. Mike said his personal best for lawsuits is 48 in one year.

He also said that he used to go "tomcatting" with Walt Disney, who told him that all women are animals. And, Mike added, he treated them accordingly. He also said that Disney was tough to work with and for.

Red Skelton was one of the most nervous comedians. Mike said that he often threw up before and after performances.

Art Linkletter, he said, was mean and a real pain to work with.

Rose Marie, from the **Dick Van Dyke Show**, insisted on bringing her dog into the work area while commercials were being filmed. Mike said that he allowed it only after she signed a liability release. The dog then urinated on the hot end of a 20,000-volt cable and… You guessed it… fried dog.

Jimmy Durante "was a prince," Mike said. He called him one of the nicest people in show business. Also, one of the ugliest.

Mike worked quite a bit with Bogart, and he said that he wrote some of the scenes for **African Queen**. He claimed credit too for providing material for Tyrone Power.

Steinbeck liked to write letters and short stories, but he didn't like to do longer works and he didn't particularly like writing as a profession. But Mike said that writing was something Steinbeck was really good at. He helped the author gather information from migrant workers in the California valleys. He said that he also assisted with the screen adaption of Steinbeck's **Tortilla Flat**, starring John Garfield.

Mike and Steinbeck used to rescue Saroyan, whom he said was a "wino." Saroyan often was arrested for rowdiness in bars. But Mike emphasized that the author never drank while he was writing. Instead, he would seclude himself.

I can identify with that.

Mike asked me to housesit for him next week, while he's in Tampa.

He's also mentioned the possibility of me doing a novel from one of his screenplays, **Break Heads, Then Feed Cats**. It would be interesting to learn more about that.

But right now, I'm not going to hold my breath for that to happen.

Who knows, though? Maybe someday I'll write a tell-all or maybe a novel loosely based on Grace, Sunny, Ellie, Mary, Mike, John, and/or my neighbor, the serial killer.

If nothing else during my nearly two years as a vagabond, I've encountered some interesting characters and been frighteningly close to what I suspect will be one of the biggest crime stories of 1978.

July 10, Tallahassee

Big news!

Doug accepted a job at a pharmacy in Miami and will go down there immediately. Grace and the girls will follow in a few weeks.

*****

Mike never went to Tampa. He followed his wife to New York City.

He had talked about going back to California and invited me to join him. I told him that I'd think about it. But no thinking about New York City required. No, thank you.

I've spent time in plenty of large cities and decided that Tallahassee is about the largest that I'd ever want to live in. Yeah, I loved Paris, but it was easy to do because I knew that I wasn't going to live there and have to deal with the traffic, noise, crowds, crime, and dog poop all over the sidewalks on a permanent basis.

Here was my introductory experience to New York City:

When Lois and I lived in Bucks County, just outside Philadelphia, we drove up there with two other couples one summer evening. They wanted to show the small-town boy the big city.

At an Italian restaurant, the waiter chased us outside, yelling obscenities. Our crime was leaving a small tip because, during the meal, he spilled water on one person and later dumped a plate of butter into the lap of another.

Yeah, wandering around Times Square and Greenwich Village was fun—as a one-time adventure. The best part occurred when one of the women in our party had to go to the bathroom and we entered a dark, smoke-filled bar. On the jukebox, Connie Francis was singing, "Who's Sorry Now?" and, as our eyes adjusted to the dim light, we noticed that only men were there. Some of them were being especially affectionate to one another. Later, after business was taken care of and we were back out on the sidewalk, I learned that wasn't a first just for me, the small-town boy. None of the others had ever been in a gay bar either.

At about 2 a.m., we returned to the Port Authority Bus Terminal, where we had parked our car. I was standing in front when the elevator door opened and a tall woman with big hair, bright red lips, and long, red fingernails stepped out with a short, fat, bald man. I noticed her nails because of what she did with them.

"Smile, sweetie!" she said, as she grabbed my lips and squeezed them together, before her partner dragged her away. I stepped onto the elevator with blood dripping from my mouth.

On our way home, my friends insisted that New York City "isn't always that bad." I laughed and said, "I'll take your word for it."

July 12, Tallahassee

Grace and Doug asked me to help her and the girls with the move and I will, of course. Mostly, I'm guessing, that means assisting with the packing and other details and then driving with them to Miami to help ensure their save arrival. He's going to start looking for a place for them to live as soon as he arrives.

*****

As I had begun to suspect over time, it now seems obvious that Mike never really had plans for Rachel's acting career and was just infatuated with her. He talked and talked about movies, TV, and commercials, and yet nothing was ever done. Then he wanted to take her to California and Grace said, "No." Thank goodness, she did.

That might be why he decided to go to New York City instead.

Over the phone, he still talks about deals with agents, plays, television series, and other show business work. But, as always, nothing is ever definitive.

Sad to say, he belongs to yesterday, but is lost in today, and I don't see how he can survive tomorrow. I doubt he ever will regain his place in Hollywood or Broadway—if he ever had a place. He's an enigma, really, and one of the cleverest men I've known. During our conversations, he took great delight in saying no one really knows him. He also spoke, almost defensively, about how "wise" he is.

Supposedly, his work has been handicapped by the IRS putting a hold on most of his assets. But he's always been ambiguous about what's going on.

He seems a generous man with friends and talked to me about the generosity of the people in his profession. Yet, he never paid musicians and actors involved in the musicals that he produced in Tallahassee. He's expressed great anguish over that. But I question his sincerity, especially since he once told me how so many other producers fold their shows without paying off debts.

Another troubling issue is that he often said negative things about the Mayfields, except for Rachel. Sometimes, I spoke up in rebuttal. Too often, I did not. One day, all that guilt I felt for keeping quiet welled up inside me and I poured it out to Grace. I've since written a letter to Mike, telling him I was wrong to keep quiet and, if we're ever together again, we won't discuss them.

Understandably, Grace was mad at me for not speaking up in her family's defense. Still, I struck back, reminding her that she had insisted I become involved with him. I think that we both feel a great deal of guilt, Grace probably more than I, since she allowed Mike to disrupt Rachel's life for more than a year with empty promises.

Now that Rachel's away from him, she's a teenager again, instead of a solemn little adult.

July 20, Tallahassee

Even though I'm there to help, Grace is not coping well with the stresses of preparing to move. And it's pretty obvious that a big part of that is Doug's absence.

As I was loading items in a tow trailer, she said, with obvious disdain in her voice, "Doug wouldn't do it that way."

If she had left it at that, I probably wouldn't have responded. She didn't.

"But you're not Doug," she added.

"Thank goodness," I replied as I avoided her eyes and continued to work.

July 22, Tallahassee

Doug wasted no time. He's found a house, and I'll drive down there with Grace and the girls in a few days.

Grace said that she and Doug want me to live with them and be a part of their family in Miami.

Wow. And I mean that in more ways than one. Yes, the invitation surprised me, although I guess it shouldn't have. They did rent a bed and put it in their living room for me while I recovered from mono.

But also, although I don't think of myself as a member of their family, I do consider them an important part of my life as good friends who provide emotional support—and possibly even the main reason that I've stayed in Tallahassee. Now they're leaving. So… if I don't accept that offer, what am I going to do?

July 24, Tallahassee

We leave for Miami in three days.

I've thought long and hard about living there with the Mayfields. But if I did, what would I do for money? Here, at least, I've got the part-time job with the **Flambeau** and the on-again, off-again work with John on his book. Yeah, I'd keep up with the freelancing in Miami, but that's not nearly enough to live on or pay my share of expenses. Of course, I always can find some kind of job for minimum wage.

But I'm nearly 30 now. It's time to decide what I want to do when I grow up, instead of continuing to be a vagabond.

July 25, Tallahassee

I realized something startling today: I've been a vagabond all my life, not just for the past two years. I went to eight different schools, including three high schools—and hated it. I'm an introvert by nature and was miserable being the new kid both my sophomore and junior years.

From birth, the longest I've ever lived in one house is four years, and that is the place where my parents live now. We moved there my junior year of high school and I lived there through junior college.

The next round of being a gypsy started when I went to Journalism School at the University of Missouri in 1968. I've been on the move since, not just since I was divorced. I've lived in five states—seven if I include my time in the Army—and had five different full-time jobs, as well as spent a year in graduate school.

So now what? Do I move to Miami with the Mayfields? Do I stay in Tallahassee? Do I go someplace else, maybe even back to place that is the closest I have to "home."

July 26, Tallahassee

I'm going home.

Yes, I'll drive down to Miami with Grace and the girls, and I'll probably even stay a couple of weeks to help them get settled, see the sights, and do a little fishing. But then I'm going back to Flat River.

Yes, I hated it when we first moved there. But family and friends from my high school and junior college days are there. And the area, in the eastern edge of the Ozarks, is rural and beautiful. I like that. Being outdoors and being able to escape people occasionally are important to me. I think that environment will be much more conducive for writing than living in Miami or staying here.

My plan is to live with my parents for as short a time as possible as I search for a place of my own. I can work the night shift as a desk clerk at the motel where Craig is employed.

And I can substitute teach. That was a possibility that I hadn't considered until my sister mentioned it. She's a secretary at the local high school, and she said that area schools always are in need. And, you know what, I just might like being a teacher. I always enjoyed school as a student, except for the moving around part.

Of course, I'll keep up the freelancing. But, I've realized, my writer friend Paul was right when he said that I'm not ready to write a novel. I'm not. I need a "sense of place" before I start trying to do that.

Grace was both understanding and apologetic when I told her. Mostly she was apologetic about the two weeks that we've been on each other's nerves while Doug was down in Miami.

She said that she thought she was hard on me because she was frustrated by our relationship. She said that she couldn't respond to me as a child, although, to me, that often seemed like what she was doing when the girls were around.

And, she added, she couldn't respond to me as a husband and lover. She couldn't hold me as she held Doug.

She told me that if she didn't have Doug, she would have married me. She said she was attracted to me in a physical way and, although she never would act on it, the feeling always was there.

Yikes! Those revelations made me even more certain I'm making the right decision. I love Grace, but am not attracted at all to her in a sexual way.

Physical separation often ends friendships over time. And that might be the case for us. But in the short term, it's going to help us sustain it, I suspect.

We'll see.

Epilogue

I kept the journal for another year, but those posts at the end of July 1978 marked the beginning of the end of my vagabond odyssey, pointing me in the direction of my life's goal: writing books.

No, I didn't get there right away. And the path wasn't linear. But it was the right one for me, and I have no regrets about moving back "home" to small-town Missouri.

I took a little longer to return than I originally anticipated. I spent more than a month in Miami with the Mayfields. I fished in the Florida Keys and visited Hemingway's home in Key West, roller skated in Coconut Grove with Linda, made some local magazine contacts, and even earned a little money as a day laborer. After I helped paint the exterior of a condo, I ate my first fried plantains, provided by the owner. I drank my first Cuban coffee and didn't sleep for 36 hours.

Back in Flat River, I started substitute teaching right away, and, my sister was right: Schools were in need and I could do it every day of the week. For awhile, I did too, strengthening my finances as I lived at my parents' for about three months.

I started working the midnight shift—11 p.m. to 7 a.m.—as a motel desk clerk about the same time I rented a mobile home on a farm outside of town. That's when I learned what sleep deprivation is all about. I'd work at the motel until 7 a.m., clean up and eat breakfast, and then substitute teach. But I was young enough to handle it—at least for awhile.

But then one night at the motel, I was so tired that I couldn't hold my head up. My body demanded sleep whether I wanted to or not. That's when I made myself cut back on the number of teaching days weekly.

When I wasn't so exhausted that I couldn't think straight, working at the motel gave me time to write too, and I made the most of it, selling feature stories to the **St. Louis Post-Dispatch** newspaper. Sometimes, the articles were about the interesting people who stayed at the motel on their way someplace else, such as the two guys using a plane to follow the migration of a peregrine falcon implanted with a small transmitter.

All of them were about nature, the outdoors, animals, and/or fishing, subjects close to my heart since childhood. Except for my short stay at Lake Ellen, I'd mostly neglected what should have been priorities in my life, but weren't for awhile there.

Back in rural Missouri, they once more were in the forefront and the realization came that my work was better and I was more prolific when my subjects were what I cared about, not what someone else wanted me to write about or what I thought I should write about. Paul had been right: I wasn't ready to write a novel. But shorter, non-fiction work flowed freely.

At the same time, I realized that I liked teaching and wanted to pursue it as well. With summers off, I reasoned, the two would blend well.

During my first year as a high school English and journalism teacher, I also sold my first article to a major outdoors magazine. Over the years, thousands would follow.

And the two careers did blend well—for awhile. In the summer, I'd travel and gather information, mostly about fishing. During the rest of the year, I'd teach and write articles.

But as I became a successful writer, selling more and more articles, inevitably the time came when I simply couldn't do both anymore. Mentally, I didn't realize it, but my body did. While practicing my role as master of ceremonies for a high school talent show, I experienced an anxiety attack as my heart started pounding and wouldn't stop.

The doctor deemed me "healthy as a horse," but said that I had to cut back. I asked for a leave of absence from teaching, but the school board refused. So, after eight years of a job that I absolutely loved, I left the world of the gainfully employed and became a full-time freelance writer.

I still hadn't written a book; I wasn't ready to. But I wrote hundreds of articles, essays, and even a few short stories annually. I traveled the world, writing about world-class fishing destinations. I became Senior Writer/Conservation for the world's largest circulation fishing magazine, **Bassmaster**, and produced an annual environmental supplement, "Living Waters."

And, by the mid '90s, I began writing my first novel. I dedicated Friday and Saturday mornings to it and set a goal of writing 2,000 words at each session. Eventually my eco-thriller, with wolves an important part of the story, began to take on a life of its own and I no longer forced myself to work on it. Each Friday, I eagerly returned to see where the action took me.

Finishing that novel provided me with one of the greatest feelings of accomplishment in my life, as did the second that I wrote soon after. The fact that I couldn't get them published was almost irrelevant, at least for awhile.

Soon, though, it weighed on me. I went to writers' conferences and talked to experts. I hired agents, who had no success on my behalf. And I learned that fiction—at least at that time—was the toughest sell in publishing.

But a friend, an attorney who decided to become an agent and represent me, suggested that I try non-fiction, especially since I had established a name for myself as a fishing/environmental writer. Within months, a major publisher accepted the first proposal that she presented on my behalf and I received a nice advance for my first book: **Better Bass Fishing**.

As of today, I'd had 14 books published, including the wolf novels. As the publishing world has changed dramatically because of technology, I've also started my own company, RUM Publishing.

Most recently, I've focused on illustrated children's books that teach kids about nature and encourage them to get outside and explore. Children, I've discovered, "are my people." So, in a way, I'm back in teaching.

Subjects for my adult books include fishing, nature, dogs, nostalgia, and the value of volunteering.

Had I moved to Miami with the Mayfields, I don't believe this ever would have happened. Yes, I probably would have continued to work at being a writer, but I'm doubtful that I would have recognized that I needed to embrace my passions to succeed. In fact, in that urban environment, I might not even have been aware of what my passions are.

Also, it was good to be close to family again, even though I've always felt I have little in common with them regarding lifestyle, interests, and beliefs, especially my parents. But we shared history and blood, and that's important too.

I was best man in my brother's wedding. I went horseback riding with my sister, and we were there for each other when she split from her husband and

I endured the hardship of a breakup from a year-long relationship. When my father died a decade after my return, I made it my mission to spend more time with my mother. In addition to helping with chores, I took her out to dinner at least weekly, and, on Sundays, she cooked breakfast for me.

Yes, I made the right decision.

And, in case you're wondering:

Sue and I got together a couple of times after we left Europe, but not right away. First, she spent more than a year in Australia, tending bar and seeing the country. In 1981, I flew to Edmonton, Alberta, and we drove more than 900 miles, much of it on gravel roads, to Yellowknife in the Northwest Territories. We visited her friends, ate caribou steaks, and went swimming in the Great Slave Lake. Even in July, the water was bitterly cold, but, once in, we didn't want to get out because mosquitoes the size of eagles waited to feast on our naked bodies.

The following year, she came down to Missouri for a week. I showed her the scenic beauty of the Missouri Ozarks and we took in a Cardinals baseball game. About a month later, she called me at 2 a.m.

"You don't love me the same way I love you," she said in a teary voice. "I'm just calling to say goodbye." And before I could respond, she hung up. When I tried to call her back, she didn't answer.

That made me very sad as I realized that she had been looking for a long-term relationship and I didn't see the signs. If I had, I would have been honest with her—at least I hope so. But again, as I've been too often in relationships, I was oblivious.

From the Bahamas, meanwhile, I continued to hear from Sunny by postcard or letter for a year or so after our split. But creditors in search of her called me long after that.

Michael Musto died in 1993, while living in Tampa, Fla. A short notice in the newspaper about his death said he "wrote Abbott and Costello's famous comedy sketch 'Who's on First' and was paid $15 for it." That suggests at least some of what he told me was true. Maybe all of it was. I'll never know.

Shortly after Ted Bundy killed two in the Chi Omega sorority, he raped and murdered a 12-year-old girl from Lake City, Fla. In 1979 and 1980, he was convicted of all three crimes and executed nine years later. He admitted to murdering 30 women, but some in law enforcement suspect the unconfirmed total is closer to 100. Also, he might never have stopped if not for that traffic stop near Pensacola, Fla., a month after the double murder in Tallahassee.

And, as investigations later revealed, one of the nation's most monstrous serial killers was, indeed, my neighbor. After taking a bus down from Atlanta, he rented a room in an old house just a few minutes' walk from my apartment and the sorority where he murdered two girls.

I continued to visit the Mayfields annually through 1984. Then in early summer of 1985, Linda came to see me. Twelve years younger than I, she had just turned 24 and was recently divorced. She obviously had sensed a connection between us that I hadn't during my visits to Miami.

I certainly did this time, though. The physical attraction for both of us was almost overpowering, and we enjoyed a wonderful week together. To be alone, we camped and hiked. We took a blanket to a scenic overlook and watched the sun rise. And during those alone times, we made love.

Not long after, I went to Florida to see her. She was in medical school, and we talked about me getting a teaching job in the area. But it was not to be. As much as I loved her—as much as I still believe she was my one, true love in this life—I couldn't bring myself to move back down there. Miami was not a place I wanted to live and, possibly even more importantly, she was recently divorced and I was just off a painful breakup a few months before.

A year or so later, Linda told me in a letter that she thought I had made the right decision, even though we loved one another.

I never married again.

Finally, I mentioned my friends Dave and Shirley a couple of times in this book. They visited me at Lake Ellen, and I visited them in Chicago. After I moved back to Missouri, they moved to the Tampa area, where David eventually became prominent as a sports information director for college and professional teams.

I visited them annually for more than 10 years, and we shared lots of good times. We rented a condo on an island for a New Year's celebration. We spent one Thanksgiving in Key West, eating shrimp instead of turkey.

Shirley confided to me that Dave considered me his best friend.

Then, on Super Bowl Sunday, 1991, Dave murdered his wife and committed suicide. He saw no other way out. He was a compulsive gambler who had squandered all of their money, as well at that he borrowed from me and other friends. Creditors were about to repossess a car and their condo, and he saw no other way out.

I could tell you more about that horrific tragedy and how it affected me for years after, but not right now. Maybe I'll include it in my next book.

[\

About the Author

Author Robert U. Montgomery started writing this book more than 40 years ago. Only he didn't know it at the time.

An unexpected divorce from a short marriage turned his world upside down. In response, he quit his job and hopped a plane to Paris. At the same time, he started keeping a journal.

Free and directionless for the first time in his life, Montgomery continued to make entries after his return, documenting adventures and misadventures, as he explored new relationships and searched for what he wanted to do when he grew up.

Through those journal entries, this book documents what he saw, experienced, and felt during those vagabond years, often with humorous insight. To provide context, Montgomery added a prologue and epilogue.

This is the author's 15th book for both adults and children. One of them was *Nourishing the Soul: The Real Value of Meals on Wheels*. He also contributed an essay to *Bright Spots: Motivation and Inspiration to Light Your Path in a Changing World*, an international bestseller.

You can learn more about the author and his works at his Amazon Author Page and at RUM Publishing, his website.

He lives in rural Missouri with his rescue dog, Pippa, who co-authored the book *Pippa's Journey*.

www.ingramcontent.com/pod-product-compliance
Lightning Source LLC
Chambersburg PA
CBHW071436080526
44587CB00014B/1866